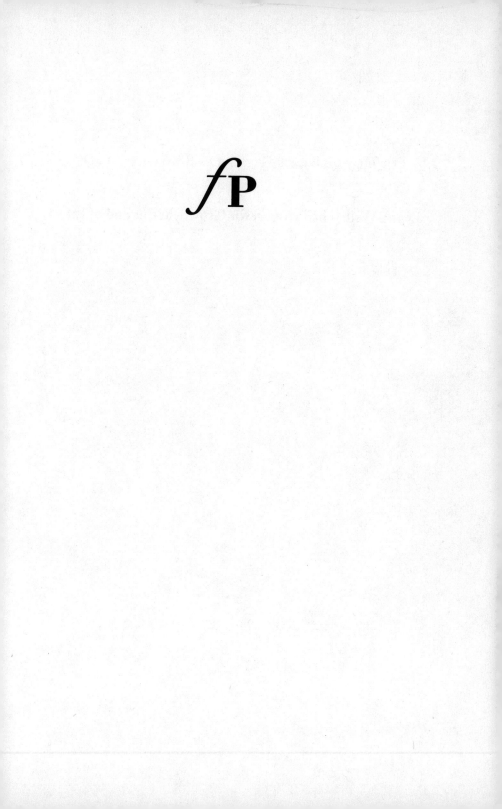

OTHER BOOKS BY IRA BYOCK, M.D.

Dying Well: The Prospect for Growth at the End of Life

The
Four Things That
Matter Most

A
Book About Living

Ira Byock, M.D.

FREE PRESS

New York London Toronto Sydney

*f*P

FREE PRESS
A Division of Simon & Schuster, Inc.
1230 Avenue of the Americas
New York, NY 10020

FREE PRESS and colophon are trademarks of Simon & Schuster, Inc.

For information about special discounts for bulk purchases,
please contact Simon & Schuster Special Sales: 1-800-456-6798
or business@simonandschuster.com

Designed by Jaime Putorti

Manufactured in the United States of America

10   9   8   7

Library of Congress Cataloging-in-Publication Data

Byock, Ira.
   The four things that matter most : a book about living / Ira Byock.
     p. cm.
   Includes index.
   1. Interpersonal communication. 2. Interpersonal relations. 3. Conduct
of life. I. Title.

BF637.C45B93 2004
158.2—dc22

2003064221

ISBN 0-7432-4909-7

To my mother,
Ruth G. Byock (1922–2003),
for giving me life and love, and teaching me what matters most.

And to my mothers-in-law, Anita Figueredo Doyle and Grada
Jansen Poirier, for helping to expand my heart and continuing to
enrich my life.

To my mother,
Ruth G. Byock (1922–2003),
for giving me life and love, and teaching me what matters most.

And to my mothers-in-law, Anita Figueredo Doyle and Grada
Jansen Poirier, for helping to expand my heart and continuing to
enrich my life.

Contents

PART ONE

The Four Things

For of all sad words of tongue or pen,
The saddest are these: "It might have been!"

JOHN GREENLEAF WHITTIER

CHAPTER ONE

Saying the Four Things

Please forgive me.
I forgive you.
Thank you.
I love you.

These four simple statements are powerful tools for improving your relationships and your life. As a doctor caring for seriously ill patients for nearly 15 years of emergency medicine practice and more than 25 years in hospice and palliative care, I have taught hundreds of patients who were facing life's end, when suffering can be profound, to say the Four Things. *But the Four Things apply at any time.* Comprising just eleven words, these four short sentences carry the core wisdom of what people who are dying have taught me about what matters most in life.

The Wisdom of Stating the Obvious

Ask a man who is being wheeled into transplant surgery or a woman facing chemotherapy for the third time what's on his or her mind and the answer will always involve the people they love. Always.

The specter of death reveals our relationships to be our most precious possessions. I've lost count of the number of times I've met people in my office, an emergency room, or a hospice program who have expressed deep regret over things they wish they had said before a grandparent, parent, sibling, or friend died. They can't change what was, but without fail their regrets have fueled a healthy resolve to *say what needs to be said before it's too late*—to clear away hurt feelings, to connect in profound ways with the people who mean the most to them.

Everyone knows that all relationships, even the most loving, have occasional rough spots. We assume that the people we love know that we love them, even if we've had our disagreements and tense moments. Yet when someone we love dies suddenly, we often have gnawing doubts.

We are all sons or daughters, whether we are six years of age or ninety-six. Even the most loving parent-child relationship can feel forever incomplete if your mother or father dies without having explicitly expressed affection for you or without having acknowledged past tensions. I've learned from my patients and their families about the painful regret that comes from not speaking these most basic feelings. Again and again, I've witnessed the value of stating the obvious. When you love someone, it is *never* too soon to say, "I love you," or premature to say, "Thank you," "I forgive you," or "Will you please forgive me?" When there is nothing of profound importance left unsaid, relationships tend to take on an aspect of celebration, as they should.

A deep, natural drive to connect with others lies at the heart of what it means to be human. The Four Things can help you discover opportunities to enliven *all* your important relationships—with your children, parents, relatives, and close friends. You need not wait until you or someone you love is seriously ill. By taking the time and by caring enough to express forgiveness, gratitude, and affection, you can renew and revitalize your most precious connections.

The Practice of Good-bye

It's been said that life is a sexually transmitted condition with a terminal prognosis. Having worked for years in close proximity to death, I have come to understand viscerally that we live every moment on the brink. We are, each one of us, at every moment, a heartbeat away from death. Seen against the backdrop of our certain mortality, our differences are dwarfed by our commonality—and the importance we hold for one another.

The stories in *The Four Things That Matter Most* are drawn from the experiences of people who have stood at death's door, and from their loved ones who learned to use the Four Things in their own daily lives. These stories inspire us to open to the potential for emotional wholeness *at any moment in our lives*—even in our most troubled relationships.

When I work with people who are approaching the end of life, I emphasize the value of saying the Four Things and I also encourage them to say good-bye. The Four Things offer essential wisdom for completing a lifelong relationship before a final parting. Thankfully, not all good-byes are final—but good-byes can be meaningful. It's important to say good-bye in a way that affirms our relationship and acknowledges our connection to one another.

The word *good-bye* derives from "God be with you," a blessing that was traditionally given at parting and, in some churches, still is. The protection and God's help of presence and guidance can be requested whether two people expect to be separated a few hours or forever. In leaving nothing unsaid, we can recapture this original meaning, so that, in saying good-bye, we are actually blessing one another in our daily interactions as well as when we face major life challenges or crises. It only takes a moment to shift the way you say good-bye from a reflex to a conscious practice. Your good-bye and your blessing can become treasured gifts to other people as you part.

Expanding the Realm of the Possible

Our world is bounded by our imagination. This may sound philosophical, but I mean it in a most practical, tangible sense. Helen Keller once wrote, "Worse than being blind would be to be able to see but not have any vision." When a formerly cherished relationship is marred by unkindness, bitterness, or betrayal, we often assume that healing is beyond our grasp, but this assumption can create a self-fulfilling prophecy. Do you really want to have such a limitation on your vision for your life?

The extraordinary experiences of the people whose stories I tell in this book demonstrate that healing and wholeness are *always* possible. Even after years of alienation, of harsh criticism, rejection, or frustration, you can establish—or re-establish—authentic understanding and appreciation of others with the help of the Four Things. Even as people confront death (their own or others'), they can reach out to express love, gratitude, and forgiveness. When they do, they consistently find that they, and everyone involved, are transformed—for the rest of their lives, whether those lives last for decades or just days. Stories and experiences of people who have courageously used the Four Things enlarge our vision and imagination, expanding the realm of the possible for us all.

Restoring Closeness

The Four Things are powerful tools for reconciling the rifts that divide us and restoring the closeness we innately desire. When bad feelings occur in our close relationships, we tend to put off the work required to make things right. We always assume we'll have another chance . . . later. That's understandable, but it's a mistake. Feeling resentful toward the people we love, or once loved, feeling distant from them, erodes our own happiness.

A brush with death often instills in us a newfound appreciation for the gift of life. Simple pleasures—a cup of tea, sunshine on one's face, the voices of our children—feel like miracles. When we've had a close call that shakes us up, the anger we've felt toward people closest to us no longer seems significant. Ill will dissolves in love, appreciation, and affection, and we recognize the urgency of mending, tending, and celebrating our relationships.

Because accidents and sudden illness *do* happen, it is never too soon to express forgiveness, to say thank you and I love you to the people who have been an integral or intimate part of our lives, and to say good-bye as a blessing. These simple words hold essential wisdom for transforming that which matters most in our lives—our relationships with the people we love.

CHAPTER TWO

The Healing Power of Words

Edwina Hargis was a patient in an ambulance speeding toward the emergency room where I was an attending physician. "Code 3," the ambulance radioed, meaning lights and sirens. "A seventy-eight-year-old woman with sudden, severe abdominal pain radiating to her back. Hypotension down to seventy by palpation."

Abrupt onset of acute abdominal pain that radiates into the back and dangerously low blood pressure can mean several things, none good: it is a classic presentation for a leaking abdominal aortic aneurysm. The diagnosis can pretty much be confirmed by a physical exam during which the paramedic feels a "pulsatile abdominal mass." In fact, that was the next thing the Emergency Medical Team reported. So I had a good idea of Mrs. Hargis's diagnosis by the time she arrived. Indeed, I had already alerted Surgery that we were getting a patient with a ruptured "triple A," and to keep an operating room open. After being stabilized in the ER, my patient would likely be coming to them STAT within 15 minutes.

When Mrs. Hargis arrived, she surprised me by saying that she was already well aware that she had an aneurysm. Furthermore, she knew it was gradually expanding and that, when it ruptured, it would be lethal. She needed major surgery to have any chance of surviving, yet other health problems—including diabetes, hypertension, coronary artery disease, and peripheral vascular disease—made it unlikely that she could survive an operation, which was the best treatment for her life-threatening condition.

I pulled up a stool to the head of her gurney. "I wish I had better news for you, Mrs. Hargis. From what you've just told me, it sounds like you understand the situation. Like a bleb on a bicycle tire, this aneurysm has been getting bigger over many months. Today it has begun to leak. As you've said, and the doctors have told you, you might well die in surgery. Without surgery you will almost certainly die within the next few hours. Do you understand?"

Mrs. Hargis had listened to my grim report with her eyes half closed. Now she nodded, as if to herself, then opened her eyes and looked at me with firm resolve. "Yes, I do," she said. She knew the score and had discussed it more than once with her internist and cardiologist. "I've known this day would come. I do not want surgery. I'm prepared."

The nurses and I were making her comfortable with medications and intravenous fluids as her family arrived in a private waiting area outside the ER.

"Mrs. Hargis, I want to let your family know what's happening. Is that all right?" I asked.

"Yes, please."

With my patient temporarily stable, I left the trauma room and met Mrs. Hargis's daughter and two sons. I explained her medical condition and her decision to decline surgery. Gently but explicitly, I informed them that without surgery her death was imminent. I was brief and to the point because I was aware of how precarious Mrs. Hargis's condition was at that moment. Time was short.

Her children were not surprised. When she had made her decision not to have surgery, almost two years ago, she had explained it to them.

As I was speaking with Mrs. Hargis's family, the nurses had cleaned the trauma room and brought in a few stools for them so that they could visit their mother until a room was ready upstairs. Before they went in, June, her eldest child, a woman in her forties, asked, "How is she doing now, doctor? And what is going to happen next?"

"At this moment, your mother is doing okay," I replied. "We're giving her pain medication and fluids. Hopefully, this will buy a little time. Let us know if you feel she is hurting too much. As the bleeding continues, her blood pressure will fall and she will become less alert. When her blood pressure falls too low, she will die. It may happen gradually, but it could be sudden. She may have only a matter of minutes or a few hours to live. I realize that this is precious family time, and we'll do all we can to preserve it."

We went into the trauma room together and I told Mrs. Hargis that I had explained the situation to her family.

Then I said, "I want to suggest something to all of you that may seem obvious, but I hope it's worth saying. Whatever time you have together today is a chance to say the things that would be left unsaid. In fact, 'stating the obvious' is important at times like this. Over the years I've learned from my patients how important it is to say four things: Please forgive me, I forgive you, Thank you, and I love you. By saying these things, people often feel better prepared to say good-bye."

"You're on the mark, doctor," said June. "Mom doesn't talk much about feelings. She loves us and I think she knows how much we love her," she looked at her mother, and then back at me. "Mom grew up in a ranching family with three brothers. They weren't outwardly affectionate. And 'I love you' was not something we said a lot to each other growing up. But there's no time like the present." She turned to her mother, "I love you, Mom!" The nurses had lowered the guardrail so June was able to lean over and hug her mother.

I excused myself, left the family, and called the operating room to tell them they could stand down. Instead of rushing to surgery, Mrs. Hargis and her family were going to use the time together to say or do whatever mattered most to them. The nurses got everyone to a private hospital room and the family asked a priest to come to administer the Sacrament of the Sick. Three hours after admission, Mrs. Hargis's blood pressure fell and she became unresponsive. A short while later she was pronounced dead.

Later that same evening, Mrs. Hargis's daughter came back to the emergency department before leaving the hospital and asked to speak with me. She said her family wanted us to know how much they appreciated the nurses' and my care of her mother. She said, "This was the best possible way for the worst possible thing to happen. My mother was a strong, stoic woman. If she had died suddenly, there would have been important things left unsaid. Your advice was so helpful. She told each of us kids how proud she was of us. That's something we had never heard her say! I told her that we would never forget her. It was stating the obvious, just as you suggested." She smiled. "Thank you for taking such good care of us all. I never realized just how much words could mean."

The words that Mrs. Hargis and her children had given one another in those last hours of her life were profound gifts. Her children will carry those blessings with them for the rest of their lives.

The Lifelong Benefits of the Four Things

Our core relationships do not, in all ways, end with death. The people who are most important to us become part of our psyche and soul. Even after their death, people who have been most central in our lives naturally continue to influence our thoughts and feelings. Saying the Four Things is important for our ongoing relationships to the people we lose through death. One day, after we die, our children and loved ones will benefit from having said the Four Things to us.

Occasionally, cynics have confronted me by saying, "It's just not that simple!" Well, it is and it isn't. I have never—and would never—imply that it is always easy to find the intimacy and warmth that we yearn for with the people who mean the most to us—or that we will all find meaning in facing our mortality. Sometimes, rather than bringing people together, serious illness pushes them apart and fractures relationships. Emotional and physical pain can try the gentlest of souls; fear can shut us down and close us off.

Yet I also know that healing and wholeness are possible—and often straightforward—even in the wake of personal troubles and tragedies, even in the face of death. I have seen them occur too many times to ignore this aspect of our human potential. And because of my work with patients of many ages, backgrounds, and life circumstances, I know that this kind of healing is not just a matter of luck. As a doctor, I cannot heal relationships between other people any more than I can will the grass to grow. I *can* prepare them for healing, plant some seeds, keep careful watch, and nurture any evidence of growth. In the plowing and planting and tending of the emotional, spiritual healing process, words are my most valuable tools. They can become yours, too.

Instruments of Healing

We often underestimate the power of words as instruments of healing. Specifically, we don't recognize the power that comes from talking with one another about our feelings and our most private, intimate fears. Here again, these sensitive subjects tend to surface when people are very sick or not expected to survive, or a loved one is about to leave on a long trip or work assignment. It's one thing to avoid talking about living wills, death, or funerals while we are playing bridge or bowling, but it's quite another to continue to avoid such subjects when an ill relative or close friend is growing visibly weaker with each visit. Culturally, we walk around the proverbial elephant in the living room without ever acknowledging the weight of separation, departure, illness, or impending death on all our lives.

Actually, we don't just avoid such conversations, we actively squelch them. It's not that we are uncaring. It's sort of automatic. Say we're with a close friend, cousin, sibling, or parent who is ill and not getting better. In the course of reviewing the recent tests, or medications, or bills, she shakes her head and mutters, "Sometimes I just wish it would be over."

"Oh, don't talk like that," we say reflexively. I've caught myself doing it, too, even with all my experience with talking and dealing with people and their lives at the end of life. It's so culturally ingrained to be optimistic and reassuring that the words are out of our mouths before we know it, like saying "Gesundheit" when someone sneezes. But we need to recognize seemingly offhand comments for what they often are—an invitation to listen. And then, perhaps, to talk.

People have often told me, "I would talk with her, but I don't know what to say." I really believe that the Four

Things will help you in such a situation. First and foremost, though, the best way to help someone who is ill, lonely, depressed, or dying is by just showing up. Being there communicates to the person how much he or she really matters to you. When you are present with someone you care about, be willing to open your mind and heart. If you are at a loss for words to say, the Four Things can help you.

The emotional and physical benefits to our health and happiness that come from connecting with others have been repeatedly demonstrated by psychological and medical research. Even our judicial system recognizes this human drive in its penal code: short of execution, solitary confinement is the worst punishment permitted by Western law. Isolation and abandonment cause suffering in people of all ages and cultures, even in the absence of illness. For people under stress, dealing with illness, or facing change, emotional isolation can be torture. Far more than pain or any other physical symptom, isolation evokes feelings of helplessness and hopelessness. This isn't only true when people are dying—it's true for everyone.

In addition to our primal drive for connection, we each have an instinctive impulse to give and receive love. We have a deep desire for healing and wholeness. Thankfully, honest, heartfelt, well-chosen words have the power to heal and make us whole. I'm not referring here to the power of prayer or chants, all of which may offer great comfort, but to the pragmatic healing potential of words like the Four Things—words that are personal but also universal.

I've seen such words rescue people from the abyss of hopelessness and despair. The Four Things have lent strength, renewed faith, and rekindled hope in the face of uncertainty. They affirm our deep connection to one another. Through well-chosen words, we can celebrate our communality, our humanity, and our individual uniqueness.

CHAPTER THREE

Completing Relationships

It is a quirk of our language that the word *complete* implies finished or over, but a relationship can be complete without ending. Conversely, a relationship may end, but remain incomplete. The word *complete* doesn't always imply finality. A circle that is complete, for instance, is whole and never-ending.

We are complete in our relationships when we feel reconciled, whole, and at peace. People say they feel complete when, if they were to die tomorrow, they'd have no regrets—they would feel they had left nothing undone . . . or unsaid.

Saying the Four Things can help us attain this sense of completion and renew the circle of our most significant relationships, reclaiming the life-affirming love from which they began. Such was the case of an Israeli couple named the Polanskys.

Overcoming Past Hurts

People who are dying recognize how fleeting and precious life is and often feel a sense of urgency about completing relationships. An Israeli grief counselor, Lynne Halamish, told me about an embittered couple in their mid-sixties, the Polanskys, for whom the Four Things proved to be a powerful tool as they grappled with her dying and their fractured relationship. In the late stages of uterine cancer, Mrs. Polansky was too ill to engage in serious counseling work and didn't have long to live. So Lynne spent most of her time with Mr. Polansky and told him about the Four Things. She had just begun when Mr. Polansky said, "Look, I can say forgive me. And maybe, because she's dying, after all, I can say I forgive you. I think I can even say thank you. But I cannot say I love you to this woman."

Lynne asked to hear the whole story. Mr. Polansky described their early relationship. "When I first met this one," Mr. Polansky said, cocking his head toward a photo of his wife in their living room, "I was absolutely head over heels in love with her. But in a very regular, constant way, she has betrayed me personally and publicly with other men over the years. Adultery. One man after another through years of our marriage. It has been a long time ago now, and so I do think I can forgive her, but I no longer love this woman—she burned that out of me. I will not tell her that I love her."

Because Lynne believes—as I do—that we gain strength from saying *all* of the Four Things, she pressed Mr. Polansky a bit. She asked him how the couple slept at night.

"Back to back, of course," Mr. Polansky told her and shrugged. She then suggested that he try something. Lynne told him that, when his wife lay asleep next to him, he could try to bring to mind the woman with whom he had been so in love. She asked him to take his time and imagine his wife as she once was. "Reconnect with her in your mind, and, if possible, in your heart," she said. "As you hold the woman you married in your thoughts and heart, whisper very, very quietly to your wife's back, 'I love you.' You don't have to do this, it's just an idea. Maybe it's a crazy idea, but it's worth considering."

Mr. Polansky was skeptical, to say the least. He asked Lynne what would happen if he said "I love you" to his wife. She confessed she didn't know and asked him, "What do you have to lose?" Lynne explained that there was little likelihood of reforming his wife in her last weeks of life, but that *he* had a lot to gain from reaching some sense of completion and closure in his marriage.

Mr. Polansky told Lynne he would think it over. As it happened, she didn't see him again before Mrs. Polansky died. She called him to extend her sympathies. A month or so later, Mr. Polansky contacted Lynne and asked if he could come see her at her office. When they met, he said he wanted to tell her what had happened.

"I did what you suggested," he began. "We were lying in bed in the dark and I closed my eyes and pictured her as she was when we met. I whispered to her back, 'I love you.' I said it to her, but I could see my young bride in the woman beside me. Before long I actually started feeling the love that I once had for her. I hadn't felt that way since I was in my thirties. After a while I woke her up and told her I loved her. And she said something to me she never said in all our years of marriage. 'You are such a beautiful man. My rock.' She put her hand on my cheek and had tears in her eyes. Then she said, 'You saved me.' We kissed, and I knew in that moment that underneath it all she had always loved me."

Lynne asked him what it meant to him to have her say that. "I got her back," Mr. Polansky replied. "The last weeks of my wife's life were the best time in the past twenty years of our marriage. I will miss her, but now I can say good-bye."

Re-creating a Lifelong Relationship

Using the Four Things as practical tools, we can deliberately decide to make our relationships whole. This can bring about a sense of completion *before* death is imminent. When we accomplish this in the relationships that matter most to us, it often opens a new chapter in our lives, as it did for Diane and Herb Cahill.

"Although my father provided well for my mom, my brothers, sister, and me, I always had the feeling we were more responsibilities to him, than a family that he really loved or wanted," Diane said in describing her relationship with her father.

When I met Diane Cahill, she was in her early fifties, tall with sandy hair and eyes highlighted by fine wrinkles at their corners from years of squinting, or smiling, in the wind and sun. I noticed her eyes because she looks directly at people when she talks. Diane had grown up in a small community north of Boise, Idaho. Her father, Herb, had been a county agricultural extension officer.

"We lived in a separate world from our father," Diane continued. She chuckled. "He was like a boarder. He would come home from work, eat dinner, then disappear into his shop in the garage. Or he would go to a local bar, play cards, and hang out with his friends. On weekends he worked in his shop—pursuing his only real interest, which was woodworking." Here Diane paused. "He *did* make my sister and me beautiful pieces of furniture, jewelry boxes, and trinkets for our birthdays and Christmas. That was his way of showing affection. But he never hugged us or expressed any warmth. In fact, he had a wicked temper. Although he never beat us (probably out of fear of what my mother would do), he occasionally spanked us, and he was always showing us 'the belt' that he kept 'just in case.'"

For most of her adult life, Diane saw little of her father. Then, at 74, Herb did an abrupt about-face. He reached out to his family and friends. "He called me up out of the blue," said Diane. "He had never done that before. And he asked to come see me. I couldn't believe it. On the phone I was flustered, almost speechless. I lived within forty minutes of him and my mom, but he'd never before taken an interest in where I was living or what I was doing. Lo and behold, the next day he came by my apartment and asked my forgiveness. I was in shock."

Diane said that he apologized to her for not having been around when she was growing up, and for not being much of a father. "For the first time in my life, he told me he loved me," she said. "You could have blown me over with a feather. He actually had tears in his eyes. He said he was proud that I had become a teacher.

"It wasn't just with me. He started going around to all of us in the family, almost everyone he knew, in fact, asking forgiveness for things he'd done or, in my case, not done.

"He told people how much they meant to him. He was very deliberate about it. He was very specific with every-one. He paid off debts—even those that had long ago been forgiven, or forgotten. I can't tell you how many people I've run into who have told me about these visits with my dad."

I asked Diane what had prompted this change.

"For a long time, we didn't know what to think. When I asked him, all he would say is, 'I figure it's time I got my life straight.'

"We were baffled, to say the least. Looking back, my mom and I have pieced together that he'd lost an old Navy friend about three months before he started making amends. Then his barber keeled over at work."

I asked Diane about her relationship with her father since his change of heart. She shook her head, as if I had missed the point.

"Only a few months later, my father died."

"Oh, so he had been ill during this time?"

"No, what's strange is that he wasn't ill at all. He was in his shop, turning the leg of a table that he was building on a lathe, and the machine blew up. It was a freak accident. My mother heard a loud bang and ran out to the garage. Dad was lying dead on the floor, his safety goggles on, pieces of the table scattered around him. We never found out what, exactly, killed him. The coroner's best guess was that he'd been electrocuted. Whatever happened, I'm certain that my father didn't know he was going to die."

"Did people give your father the forgiveness he sought? Did you?"

"Oh, yes," said Diane. "He was *so sincere*. It may sound funny, but I was actually happy for him. He was softer, more genuine. We had such a wonderful time those few months. We had a real father-daughter relationship for the first time. It was a shock to lose him so soon after he had reached out to us. The whole family was devastated. But, without a doubt, it was easier because of what we had all shared in those preceding months. My mother feels the same way. When she talks about him, she's sad, but she's told me that she also feels proud of him—as if in some way *he made it!* We all got the feeling that he was content with himself before he died, probably for the first time in his life."

I asked Diane if she thought there were any lessons in her father's story that she would carry with her. She thought for a moment. "I never realized just how much was missing in my life until my father reached out to me. It was as if something that was broken inside me suddenly felt whole. I know he felt the same way. There was a deep sense of peace and warmth. I guess the lesson for me is that it's never too late to say what needs to be said," she said. "But it is also never too early. Because you just never know."

Diane and her family took to heart the lessons of the last

days of her father's life. To this day, they make sure they say the Four Things to each other regularly.

Coming Current in Your Relationships

Interestingly, people who are physically well often feel the same pressing need to complete relationships as people who are dying. You don't need a grave diagnosis or a brush with death to "come current" in your relationships. Herb had the right idea. We never know when we're going to die. Completing our relationships by saying the Four Things to the people who mean the most to us is a way of reaffirming and invigorating what's truly important in our lives.

By saying the Four Things, Mr. Polansky experienced a sense of completion and closure with his wife that he never dreamed possible. He was able to reawaken feelings for her that he thought were long dead, but were, in fact, actually dormant.

For both the Polanskys and the Cahills, completion meant closing a circle that had been broken. When serious disruptions have impaired the connection between people, completion means acknowledging rifts, recognizing difficulties, and reconciling relationships. In both cases, a family's life was transformed and the legacy left was marked by joy rather than pain. And part of that legacy is a resolve to maintain and renew loving connections with other people in their ongoing daily lives.

CHAPTER FOUR

Transformations

Whenever we are able to open up and become vulnerable and honest with ourselves, we allow the opportunity for profound transformation. People who acknowledge that their lives may soon be over tend to have little patience with pretense, including their own. In the naked honesty that accompanies death's approach, many people feel a *need* to apologize for having been self-centered, irresponsible, or just plain wrong.

Most people who are dying still have the capacity to change in ways that are important to them. Their transformation can also make an enormous, and lasting, difference to the people around them. Even the least introspective person may begin to look inward. Serious illness can allow people to experience the immediacy of life. Hard, angry, suspicious people (who, it seemed, would stay that way to the bitter end) often soften, becoming vulnerable and even trusting. I look at these changes not as deathbed conversions, but as quantum leaps in personal development—opportunities to achieve a state of mind and an intimacy with others that might not otherwise come to pass.

We know that our family and friends are the most important parts in life, but we tend to get distracted, enmeshed as we often are in the work and family responsibilities that fill our daily lives. Saying the Four Things *before* we or they confront eternity is a way to honor and affirm the primacy of our relationships. The Four Things help us align our words and deeds to what matters most.

In my public talks and clinical workshops, I have often used Steve Morris as a case to illustrate how the Four Things can point us toward this type of transformation.

Becoming Well Within Yourself

When our hospice team met Steve, he was dying hard. Struggling for every breath, he was unable to walk without gasping for air, yet unable to sit still because of the anxiety that defined his life. Steve was scared of dying, and he suffered through every waking moment of every day.

By vocation Steve had been a lineman for the phone company before a heart attack and emphysema forced him into retirement. By avocation he was a real Montana cowboy, living for his horses, winning numerous riding competitions and the affection of many for his willingness to teach horsemanship to any child eager to learn. In appearance and in his lifelong smoking habit, Steve was also the prototypical Marlboro Man. A man's man, he was not one to express emotions or even admit to having them. More often than not, work and his horses had come before relationships—and family.

Now he was at the end of his rope. The specialists had exhausted every hope of cure, including hope for the lung transplant he had desperately sought. Steve was the one dying, but he was not the only victim of his condition. His wife, Dot, was his constant companion, nurse, handmaiden, and cosufferer. If she were out of his sight for more than a minute, he would ring his bell or utter a dampened shout in high-pitched panic, "Dot. *Dot!*"

It took our hospice team two weeks and a combination of pharmacology, counseling, and pragmatism to gain Steve's confidence. We were meticulous in giving him medication to relieve anxiety and tension. We also taught him to use relaxation tapes, and made suggestions regarding placement of his recliner that helped him breathe easier and not feel so isolated. We had hospice volunteers relieve Dot of caregiving for an hour or two here and there so that she could shop for groceries, see her own doctor, and get a few moments of rest. All our efforts, drawing on our experience and resources of palliative care, helped diminish—at least slightly—Steve's breathlessness and paralyzing fear.

As we learned more of Steve's personal history, however, we realized that his anxiety stemmed in part from the fractured nature of several key relationships and the complex, conflicted nature of his family's life.

One Thursday, while I was visiting Steve and Dot at their home, we talked about his relationships with his family, about some of his regrets, and about his wishes for the people he loved. Then I taught him about the Four Things.

"Before any significant relationship is complete, before it's brought full circle," I said, "people have to say four things. Please forgive me, and I forgive you—because if this was a significant relationship, there will always be some history of hurt between them. Thank you. And I love you."

"Those are really good, Doc." Steve responded with unexpected enthusiasm. "Write those down for me, will ya?" he asked in his muffled, gravelly voice.

Using one of the 3 x 5 cards that I kept in my shirt pocket for jotting myself notes, I wrote the Four Things. Before leaving, I scheduled another visit in five days.

When I arrived the next Tuesday at noon, Dot stood waiting for me behind the glass storm door of the entry to their home. Steve and Dot were clearly eager to relate the events of the past weekend. On Sunday their children and grandchildren had come over for dinner. As they assembled around the table, Steve had announced that he had some things he needed to say. He began, "You know the doctors tell me that this emphysema is finally going to get me. And I know I haven't always been the best father, or husband. Well, there are some things I want to say." With his eyes on my handwritten list, he said the Four Things in his own words.

The effect on everyone there was remarkable. Although Steve's anxiety did not disappear, its grip weakened on him in the wake of his remarks. When he asked forgiveness from the people he cared most about, he said that he had suddenly felt transformed. He was able to tell them how much they meant to him and how much he loved them. Steve's life didn't become easy, but it did become less anguished. After that day, everyone reported that there was now a tenderness and a cohesiveness among them that no one could remember having felt before. One of Steve and Dot's adult daughters told me that this was the first time in their lives together that she and her siblings were able to show affection openly to their father.

As he faced his life's end, Steve was transformed and so was everyone around him. He was happier with himself than he could ever remember being, he said. Paradoxically, in the process of dying, he was healing and becoming well within himself. And in healing his own emotions, he helped his children heal theirs—for the rest of their lives.

Filling the Void

Transformations of this magnitude in response to saying the Four Things are not isolated or rare.

One day, I told Steve's story during a lecture at Johns Hopkins University. Afterward, a large, middle-aged black man came toward me as I was leaving the auditorium and surprised me by abruptly embracing me. At first I was taken aback. People were filing from the hall and here I was enveloped by an obviously emotional man, twice my size. He explained that he served as a chaplain at an inner-city public hospital in Baltimore and needed to tell me his story. Like many of the most affecting stories that I've heard over the years, it was about transformation at the very end of life.

A few months earlier, the chaplain had been paged to the bedside of a 33-year-old man who was dying of AIDS. Just two hours earlier the patient, Antoine, had found out that he had a teenage daughter and that she was on her way to the hospital to see him.

"I was terrified about saying the wrong thing," said the chaplain. "I thought, 'Why me? What can I possibly do that would be of any help?' Then I remembered about saying 'the Four Things.' I was present for Antoine's and his daughter's meeting and used the Four Things to guide their visit. Antoine needed little encouragement, or help, to ask, 'Can you forgive me?' and to say, 'Thank you for coming to see me,' and 'I love you' to this frightened, anxious 15-year-old girl. And Chantelle, who really does have her father's eyes, was able to say, 'Thank you for being my father'; 'Of course, I forgive you'; and then, 'Daddy, I love you, too.'

"They visited for just over an hour, each hungry to ask questions and tell stories. There were lots of tears; it was hard to separate the tears of sadness from those of joy. Ultimately, Antoine's fatigue and breathlessness forced their visit to end. They kissed each other as they said good-bye."

Listening to this story, I was trembling, but the chaplain wasn't done. "I checked on Antoine later that evening and found out he had died within three hours of the visit."

This work will keep you humble.

Measuring Your Time by Its Depth, Not Its Length

Antoine's life had been transformed in his last hours—he died knowing that he had a daughter, a daughter who loved him. Chantelle's life was also changed forever. She now knows she had a father who loved her, who saw her as she was. He apologized, asked for her forgiveness, and she willingly gave it. She misses all that could have been, but feels fullness in her heart where there had previously been emptiness and pain.

Many people come to the end of their life with fractured relationships. But as the stories of Herb, Steve, and Chantelle show, the healing of a broken relationship in the last hours, or even minutes before death, can reframe the history of the relationship and the biographies of everyone involved. The Four Things can help us be honest and open. They present an extraordinary opportunity, one that is available to us all to use in our lives to heal any relationship, any day.

Of course, not all relationships are fractured. Sometimes, our only regret is death's relentless approach or another parting of ways. In these cases, the Four Things offer a way of expressing sadness over the loss of a shared future and rejoicing over the gift of a shared past. By employing the Four Things in such circumstances, you measure time not in length, but in depth.

In situations in which time is extremely short, being prepared to say the Four Things can help make the best of the worst situation. Sometimes the Four Things come to us naturally, especially the need and desire to say, "I love you."

The people trapped on the upper floors of the World Trade Center and in the highjacked planes on September 11, 2001, called their loved ones to say it one last time. It was the most important call they ever made. Saying "I love you" and expressing the spirit of the Four Things is a priceless gift for those who live on. The knowledge of being loved, even when you are separated from each other, sustains you and provides you with inner strength and comfort.

PART TWO

Forgiveness

Forgiving presupposes remembering. And it creates a forgetting not in the natural way we forget yesterday's weather, but in the way of the great "in spite of" that says: I forget although I remember. Without this kind of forgetting no human relationship can endure healthily.

PAUL JOHANNES TILLICH

Introduction

People's need to feel forgiven—and to forgive—is a recurring lesson in every spiritual tradition. It has certainly been one of the main lessons I've learned in my own work. People who are dying have shown me that our human capacity to forgive and to be forgiven is enormous. Their experiences reveal the practical power of forgiveness to enrich the lives of the people they leave behind.

In *The Tibetan Book of Living and Dying,* Sogyal Rinpoche writes: "All religions stress the power of forgiveness, and this power is never more necessary, nor more deeply felt, than when someone is dying. Through forgiving and being forgiven, we purify ourselves of the darkness of what we have done, and prepare ourselves most completely for the journey through death."

We do not have to wait until we or someone we love is dying to practice forgiveness. The stories in this section of the book span situations that call for forgiveness even when it seems impossible. These stories suggest strategies to complete even the most deeply wounded relationship.

Many people confuse forgiveness with exoneration. Forgiveness does not excuse someone from doing something wrong. It does not alleviate their guilt or lessen their transgression. Instead, forgiveness accepts the past as it was, embraces the present, and faces the future. Forgiveness is a strategy for you to become free of emotional baggage. Hate, fury, recrimination, and blame weigh us down. The ball and chain of old wounds tethers us to the past and limits our ability to move forward with vitality.

CHAPTER FIVE

Loved Ones Live On Inside Us

"Please forgive me" and "I forgive you" can be the toughest two of the Four Things to say. And yet few of us will live a full life without the need to say both. The need to forgive and be forgiven simply means that we're not perfect. If we listen to our hearts we know that in the relationships that matter most there will often be instances of anger or, at least, serious misunderstandings that cause hurt. Sometimes the bad things and bad feelings that happen between people are more serious. One doesn't have to be Sigmund Freud or Frasier Crane to realize that we live in a world filled with people in emotional pain.

My years of clinical work in palliative care and in emergency medicine have driven home, again and again, that, as we grow up and age, each of us is emotionally scarred to some extent. Most of these injuries heal, but some don't. These sore spots may be as mundane and beyond our control as feeling that we never lived up to a father's unreasonable expectations, or that we aren't tall enough or pretty enough. We might blame ourselves for never having followed or fulfilled a lifelong dream. Some old wounds from our youth may be mostly closed—or so we think, until a careless, casual remark by a parent, sibling, or close friend "picks the scab" and reminds us of the hurt we still carry. The wounds associated with infidelities, lies, divorces, libels, and lawsuits tend to be open and obvious. And many people also carry wounds carved by physical, emotional, and sexual abuse.

It is no surprise then that forgiveness is so often at the heart of completing relationships and finding peace. We may need to forgive in order for the relationship to continue and we may need to forgive to close the relationship in a healthy way. Forgiveness is a passage to a sanctuary of wholeness, that nurturing place where we feel intimately connected to the people who matter most to us. It is a place of healing and transformation. In it, we feel the perfect fullness of the present.

Emotional Healing

In medicine, healing refers to restoring a person to a natural state of health and wholeness. Physical wounds occur when an accident or injury disrupts the integrity of a person's skin and subcutaneous tissue. In cleaning the wound of dirt and infected tissue, the natural wisdom of the body is able to reestablish the tissue's integrity. When it does, we say that the wound is healed.

A similar process occurs with emotional wounds. Healing is effected when the toxic material in the rift between two people has been cleansed and they are able to reestablish a sense of closeness. Forgiving is an act of cleansing that enables the wisdom within us to reach out and reconnect with people we once loved.

One night over dinner, Carla, an old friend, and I were discussing my ideas for this book about saying the Four Things before good-bye. She told me a powerful story of forgiveness and its potential to transform us.

"The Sweetest Man"

Carla is a successful architect from Chicago, the wife of my friend Julian. Her father had died ten years earlier of pancreatic cancer, just as my father had.

"Dad was dead in less than two weeks from his first real symptoms," said Carla. "He was the sweetest man in the world—and one of the most unhappy."

Carla's description of growing up in the suburbs west of Boston in the 1950s evoked the kind of American family depicted in the Chevrolet ads of that era: her father in a checkered shirt, sweater vest, and dark slacks, smoking a pipe while he watered the lawn; her mother in a cardigan and pleated skirt, waving from the front door, holding a freshly baked pie; Carla playing hopscotch on the front walk and her younger brother, Paul, pulling his red Radio Flyer wagon; a happy active home life that revolved around bright, well-groomed children.

Carla's father, Anthony Fornataro, was a hands-on father years before it was in vogue. By all appearances, he was
successful and happy, and part of him undoubtedly was. He
made a good living selling high-end orchestral instruments
and reveled in hearing them played.

When he was young, Anthony had been a serious musician, a cellist who practiced tirelessly in hopes of earning a
chair in the Boston Symphony Orchestra. That was before
the Depression put the cost of lessons out of reach and
World War II infantry duty in France made practicing impossible. After the war he took a job with an instrument
company, temporarily he thought, but then he married and
Carla came along, and his priorities changed.

Carla said she thought her father never really got over
his lost dream of being a symphony musician. He always
wrestled with his past and struggled inside himself with
who he was and who he might have been. Carla said he
bristled at the stereotype of Italian-Americans. He was
physically big and burly, yet he was one of the best educated
and most refined men she had ever known. A sure way to
get him angry was to make jokes about the Mafia. He never
let anyone call him Tony. He was Anthony, even to his closest friends.

Carla hadn't realized how troubled her father was until
she was in twelfth grade, when she found out that he was
drinking secretly. Although she didn't know how long it
had been going on, it was obvious to her during her college
years that he was sick and depressed. Paul caught more of
the brunt of it, because he was younger and still lived at
home. Carla described scenes out of *Who's Afraid of Vir-*

ginia Woolf? when her parents visited her while she was in graduate school in New Haven.

"We'd go out to dinner," she said, "and they would start drinking, arguing, and yelling awful things at each other in public. At first, I couldn't believe that this was my family. But it became almost predictable.

"My father and I were always extremely close. We had a very special relationship. Dad really introduced me to art and design, and I shared his passion for music. It seems strange and even a bit unhealthy now, but when I was in college, we spoke on the phone almost every day, especially during his bouts of depression."

I asked Carla if her father had ever sought help for his depression from a doctor or therapist. She explained, "The summer between my sophomore and junior years of college, we had actually all gone to family therapy. The therapist had us 'stage' a play of our family. She gave us situations and we acted our roles. Dad was always center stage. He was the center of the family, and in many ways the core of our problems. Not that it was his fault. It wasn't intentional, but he took a lot of energy."

One day in February when Carla was 28 and in architectural school, she received a panicked call from her mother. Anthony had become violently ill, and had had to be rushed to the hospital. Carla raced home to be with her parents.

"When I got to the hospital," Carla said, "Dad was in a semiprivate room on the second floor, under the care of his internist and good friend Sidney Levinson. By the next afternoon, the tests, including a CAT scan, showed that there was a tumor on his pancreas."

Pancreatic cancer is deadly. By the time it is diagnosed, it is almost always too late to cure surgically, and no good treatment yet exists to stem its progression. The pancreas is usually an unassuming organ, quietly going about its mundane tasks of releasing insulin and other hormones into the bloodstream to regulate blood glucose and excreting enzymes into the duodenum to aid in digestion. Pancreatic cancers are rarely large but most are strategically located to cause maximum trouble, sitting at the juncture of the ducts draining the pancreas's own enzymes and bile from the liver into the duodenum.

As they grow, pancreatic tumors can obstruct the flow of bile or keep food from passing through the intestine. Sometimes palliative surgery can help bypass those blocks, and occasionally chemotherapy and radiation therapy can slow the progression of the tumor. In Carla's father's case, medication for pain and vomiting, IV fluids, and "GI rest"—allowing his stomach and intestines a couple of days off from their constant chores of digesting and absorbing nutrients—were all that was urgently needed. "Sid had a local oncologist see Dad," Carla said, "but there wasn't much to be done. So, I'd just sit long hours with him."

Paul was in the midst of exams, and scheduled to come a few days later, and Carla's mother was dealing with some less serious medical issues of her own. So Carla spent a good amount of time alone with her father. "I would read to him, from the newspaper, and from a biography I had with me," Carla said. "And I would lie on his bed with him and we'd just talk about anything and everything. This went on for a few days. He was too sick to go home, and he couldn't eat; yet he was fairly comfortable. Some days we'd act as if nothing was wrong. It wasn't that we were denying what was happening, we'd just choose not to dwell on it. I couldn't really deny how bad things were, though. I remember watching him sitting up in his hospital bed trying to write a letter. He couldn't. His hand wasn't steady enough. Knowledge and academic achievement were so much a part of who Dad was to himself. Well, I knew it was a sign of the coming defeat."

As pancreatic cancer grows, the tumor sends out chemical messengers that disrupt energy metabolism within cells throughout the body. The result is that patients with pancreatic cancer may look as if they are being consumed from within, just as "consumptive" or tubercular patients do. They progressively lose weight and become terribly weak as energy that is normally available to maintain muscle mass and activity is sapped.

"But those days were also an incredible time," said Carla. "Dad was actually more calm and composed than I can ever remember seeing him. He knew how difficult he'd been through the years. We certainly said the Four Things, lots of 'I forgive you's and 'I love you's, that's for sure."

"Did he actually apologize to you?" I asked, "or was it just implied?"

"It was more than implied. He said, 'I'm sorry.' He talked about how tough it had been for him and how emotionally sick he had been, and how difficult it had been *for me*. He apologized for being so needy. And I apologized for not being able to make it all better for him. I think that was the hardest thing for me as a person who loved him so much."

"Did he ever leave the hospital?"

"Actually, he did come home for all of three days. He got out of Valley View on Saturday. I left that Sunday evening to go back to New Haven for a couple of days."

"It must have been hard for you to leave."

"It was hard, but by then we had said everything. We were on a whole new level of being together. His asking my forgiveness seemed to open up a deep well of tenderness in me. I just told him again how much I loved him and said again that I forgave him for everything. I said I'd see him on Thursday. And we hugged for what felt like hours. He said, 'I love you, too, Miss Carla'—that's what he called me. So, I definitely had precious opportunity to say the Four Things, and good-bye, to my dad. It was a very hard and a very wonderful thing."

Carla's father died just two days after she left, sooner than anyone expected.

"What about your brother?" I asked. "Do you have a sense of whether or not he was able to come to some sense of completion with your father?"

"I've always felt bad for Paul because he didn't have the same quality of time I did with Dad that last week," Carla reflected, shaking her head. "I think that in a lot of ways he's still wrestling with Dad inside himself."

Carla recalled a painful scene before she left Boston. The Celtics basketball game was on TV and Paul really wanted to watch it with his father. "Dad was just too ill, and simply not interested. But Paul's feelings were hurt and they argued. Paul's disappointment over the game echoed the times in his teenage years that Dad couldn't be there for him, because of his depression. It tapped into Paul's well of resentment. Then Dad died before they could talk through it. I don't think Paul has ever entirely gotten over his anger toward Dad."

The Ongoing Power of Memories

The contrast between Carla's and her brother's experience of their father's dying is striking. Also striking is the different feeling each has of the personal, ongoing relationship with the memory of their father.

"People live on within us" is not just a pleasant nostrum from a Hallmark card or a metaphysical assertion. In tangible ways, our relationships with the people we have lost through death continue. It's natural for the most important people in our lives—our parents, brothers and sisters, spouses, children, and our closest friends—to become part of who we are. Death can't change that; even death is not that strong. In many ways, both conscious and unconscious, people continue to influence our everyday perceptions of the world and our sense of ourselves. And they continue to populate our dreams at night. They are an entirely normal, important part of our psyche and as such, they do live on within us.

From a psychological perspective, it is possible to complete relationships with people who have died. Most often, however, it's a lot easier to do so when they are alive.

Carla and her father brought their relationship to completion. She still draws comfort from the sense of resolu-

tion she and her father achieved. In contrast, Paul's experience is marked by a sense of things unresolved. He didn't
have the chance to talk with his dad the way that Carla had.
And their father never had the opportunity—or didn't take
the opportunity—of saying to Paul some of the things, including "I'm sorry," and "Please forgive me," that he had
said to Carla. Paul loved—and still loves—his father deeply.
Most maddening for him is the feeling that things might
have been resolved. Paul is caught between being unable to
deny residual resentment toward his father and feeling
small for the anger he carries because he realizes his father
was as powerless against his depression as he was against his
final illness.

Resolving this relationship may still be possible, but it is
more difficult and typically takes much longer. In order to
feel a renewed sense of connection with his father, Paul
may have to find some way to feel that forgiveness, appreciation, and love have been sent, and received. A skilled
counselor or spiritual teacher can help.

More than likely, in order for Paul to feel whole in his
relationship with his father, he will also need to forgive
himself. Like the rest of us, he will need to accept himself as
he is—mistakes, regrets, and all—and go forward with
compassion and love for himself and others. Truly forgiving yourself is not easy in a culture that strives for perfection, but it is something all of us should practice.

Learning that someone in our life is seriously ill can wake
us to the need to say the things that would be left unsaid if
death came suddenly—to either of us. Whether we make

use of that opportunity—or not—can affect our life for years to come.

Carla is emphatic in applying the lessons from her experience with her father to her relationships with her son and daughter. "Every day I make sure my children know how much I love them for who they are. When they were younger, especially after we'd had an argument, before they went to bed I'd take them by the shoulders, look in their eyes, and say, 'I love you.' To this day, every time I take a plane or train, I leave a note telling them where I'll be and when I'll be home. Every note ends with, 'I love you to infinity and back.'

"I've written letters to each of my children that are in our safe–deposit box. I tell them how much I love and am proud of them, and how confident I am in the choices they'll make in life. I wrote, 'If we were having an argument just before I died or if there are things left unresolved between us, you can be sure that I know that our disagreements are tiny in comparison to our love. Please forgive me for not always understanding and for nagging and worrying too much. Being your mother is the best thing I ever did!'"

Carla's relationships with her children are healthy, and she strives to keep them complete on a daily basis. She does this because it is a practice in family wellness and in being present for them, in being there for them. But it is also a beautiful way of honoring her father and the lessons of his difficult life.

CHAPTER SIX

Resolving a Legacy of Pain

Anger, blame, guilt, and regret cause pain that divides people who love each other or want to love each other. The words *Please forgive me* and *I forgive you* can be the bridge that reestablishes connection and allows healing to happen.

Jennifer Matesa, a fellow writer, graciously offered the wisdom of her relationship with her mother and their final days together in a story she told me one afternoon.

Jennifer had always hoped to hear "Please forgive me" from her mother, but Mary projected an authoritative, not particularly affectionate air. Her mother rarely admitted being wrong or making an error in judgment—and her mother never said, "I'm sorry."

Dropping Pretense in Order to Heal

At 58, Mary was diagnosed with cancer that had spread to her brain. After the diagnosis was confirmed, Mary's oncologist told her that there was nothing he could do except refer her to hospice for palliative care in order to improve her comfort and the quality of her life.

"What he *didn't* tell my mother," Jennifer said, "was that she would lose her sight, her hearing, her ability to speak, her balance, and her mental capacity. He also didn't mention that the cancer from her lung was now burning its way through her central nervous system and that she would experience seizures. During the seizures she would lose track of her thoughts and words. She would stare intently at some invisible person or scene, or perhaps at nothing at all."

Since these staring spells were not grand mal seizures, in which people fall to the floor convulsing, sometimes no one would notice when they occurred. One day, during a seizure, Mary left the water running in the kitchen sink while making her husband's breakfast; the drain plug was in, and he caught the tap just as the sink was about to overflow. All the while Mary was staring vacantly at an open cupboard. Another morning, without realizing it, she put out four slices of toast and an English muffin for him to eat. Jennifer's father made a joke about his appetite to cover the awkward moment, but the incidents of Mary's "going away" were poignant and telling, nonetheless.

The oncologist also never instructed Jennifer or her family to monitor her mother's vital signs during seizures.

Once, when she'd "gone away," her mother had a pulse racing at more than 200 beats per minute, the result of a sustained burst of adrenaline from her adrenal glands' reflex response to the stress of the seizure in her brain. Jennifer and her brother were shocked and immediately called 911. All the while, their mother's face was fixed in a faraway, seraphic half-smile.

Fortunately, Jennifer and her parents lived in the same city and she tried to visit them every day. Throughout her mother's illness, their relationship had been mutually supportive, even friendly, but not overtly affectionate. It became clear to Jennifer that her mother, although only 58, was going to die soon, so Jennifer had spoken to a counselor who advised her, "Get it clear between you if you can. You only have so much time. You need to hear that she loves you or you will regret it for the rest of your life." Jennifer decided to go for it.

One afternoon, Jennifer and her small son arrived to find Mary working in fits and starts on her goddaughter's First Communion dress, trying to apply a large bow to the back of the waist. At this point, Mary was almost deaf, and her right eye wandered; she struggled with the slippery synthetic satin, lace, and tulle. She'd forget her place, then doggedly pick up from where she'd left off. The dress would be her hands' last work. She worked on it in silence.

As she watched her mother, Jennifer weighed her words, then dived in.

"Mom," she asked, "do you want me here? Are you happy when I come to visit?"

Mary raised her eyes to her daughter's face, a sewing

needle held between her teeth. Her weight loss and near-baldness gave her a "plucked-chicken" look, Jennifer said, but she was able to recognize her mother's beauty—her dark brown eyes, set at a tilt; her high cheekbones and sweetly pointed nose.

"It's been hard between us," Mary told her slowly. "We've spent so many bad times that I don't think we know where or how we stand with each other."

Her mother struggled to find words amid the damage the cancer had wrought; she talked haltingly about needing to take the time to "rebuild things" so that they could have "better times." Jennifer recognized that her mother was searching for a way to convey her feelings. Jennifer hung on every word, hoping her mother's mental clarity would not give out.

"Mom never apologized or said, 'I made mistakes and I am sorry; please forgive me,'" Jennifer told me. "Instead she used the passive voice—'There were mistakes,' she said. I knew what she meant, though. It took a lot of strength to relinquish her pride and pretense of motherly perfection and acknowledge even that mistakes had been made. She was beginning to speak of her sorrow, in her proud way, and in perhaps the only way she could find in her illness."

"When I imagine dying," Jennifer continued, "I always imagine being lucid till the end. Isn't that what we're all afraid of: confronting death with a lucid mind, a clear eye? But how much more terrifying it must be to feel yourself slipping from life without being able to speak, see, hear, or even think.

"So Mom and I talked about our relationship. I told her that I felt for her because of the way she had been raised—in a cold, hard home full of work and fear. This was the first time I'd ever told her I felt any compassion for her. I think she recognized that I was apologizing for the many times I snapped at her impatiently or judged her unfairly. Her eyes grew distant again, but I realized she was not going away; she was looking back into her childhood.

"Then she said, 'I don't know why anyone should have to grow up with such a level of . . .' She faltered, and I worried that the thought was eluding her. 'Hatred,' she finished simply. 'And anger,' she added. 'My own mother was . . .' I thought this time that she really had lost the thought. What had her mother been? Seconds passed. 'A destructive force,' she said, with finality."

Jennifer asked her mother what they could do to become closer. Was there anything they could say? It was then that her mother apologized, in another way.

"'I know I passed things to you that my mother passed to me, that were destructive,' my mother stammered slowly. I was absolutely astonished. It was true, and I had longed to hear her say so, but I had no idea my mother knew it, or felt that way. Again, I prayed that she wouldn't lose track of the thought."

Jennifer watched her mother's eyes search intensely beneath her tightly knitted brow before she spoke again. "She said, 'I know that you are the way you are, because I am the way I am, because my mother was the way she was.'"

This crystallized an idea that Jennifer had worked for years to understand: the hatred and anger, the physical punishment, the screaming, the criticism, the name-calling, the days and days of cold-shoulder treatment she had experienced as a child were not her fault as much as they were a painful legacy passed blindly down through the generations.

But her mother was letting it go, and Jennifer wondered if she could, too.

"'I don't have to be that way anymore. There is no longer time enough to be that way,' my mother said, and then, after another concentrated pause, she added, 'It's going to stop with him,' and she pointed a finger toward my eighteen-month-old son who was playing with blocks on the floor, blissfully unaware of what was transpiring. 'The bad stuff can stop,' Mom told me, 'but the good stuff can be passed on. That's what I want us to do.'"

Jennifer told me that her mother's frankness enabled her to say that she was sorry if she had been stingy with her affection or appreciation toward her mother. Her mother replied that she did not feel that way. In so few words, layers and years of hard feelings melted away.

Then, with great effort, Jennifer's mother rose stiffly and put her arms around her daughter.

"'You are the artist of my life. I am so proud of you,' she told me."

"I held her close to me and thanked her. I took the satin and pins out of her hands. And that evening, I spent five hours finishing her work on that dress."

With the help of hospice, and the constant care of Jennifer, her father, her brother, and her sister, Jennifer's mother died some six weeks later, peacefully, in her own home.

I wondered what Jennifer thought were the main lessons of her remarkable experience with her mother.

"Some people might think that the words we shared as mother and daughter that day were too little and too late," she said. "It would have been better if Mom and I never needed to have such a conversation. But family life is messy, filled with loose ends that are rarely tied up in bows.

"Here is what I know," she continued. "My mother died three and a half years ago and hardly a day has gone by that I have not recalled her words to me, and mine to her, at her kitchen table that day. Every day I recall the responsibility I bear. If the anger and hatred is in fact to stop with me, and my son is to be free of it, I am the one who must stop it. In turn, that begins with the way I treat myself. That was the gift that hearing my mother's sorrow gave me: the permission—the requirement—to begin to treat myself with patience, acceptance, and love, and so to treat others likewise. To begin to forgive her. And in forgiving her, in a deeper way than I can articulate, I begin to forgive myself. I now know there is no longer time enough to be any other way."

Forgiveness Establishes a Positive Legacy

Jennifer and Mary's story demonstrates the power and healing potential of forgiveness. Painful legacies can arise from damaging emotional patterns that are perpetuated from generation to generation. As one damaging emotion gives rise to the next, a destructive pattern can result, like the jarring, punishing washboard ridges in a dirt road. Forgiveness is a courageous way of saying, "Enough is enough!" It requires us to confront the imperfections and pain of the past, not ignore or excuse them. Once we can see them and their origins with compassion, we can again experience the love that is our birthright. With love we can pave a future that is healthy and whole.

CHAPTER SEVEN

The Emotional Economics
of Forgiveness

It is easy to forgive someone for something done inadvertently, especially if you are close to that person and have been all your life, as Carla was with her father, but how can we forgive someone who has intentionally done us serious harm? When a parent or other loved one has been loving and supportive, the inadvertent hurt is a small glitch in an otherwise beneficial relationship, but how do we work to forgive repeated, purposeful offenses? To be honest, I don't have an absolute answer to this question. Sometimes people simply can't find it within themselves to forgive each other. But I have learned a few emotional strategies for approaching forgiveness in particularly difficult situations that have helped others.

The first strategy turns on accepting that we're just

human. And that means we screw up from time to time (some of us more often than others). Most of the time when people are nasty, mean-spirited, or greedy they are acting out their own pain.

As a physician I have seen the devastating effects that physical pain can have on people's lives. Acute pain, at least, sometimes protects us. We instantly remove our hand from a hot stove and remember to check before putting it there again. In contrast, chronic pain has no biological purpose. It can make proud, productive people feel useless and isolated. Whether it is daily migraines or relentless back pain, physical suffering captures a person's attention and doesn't let go. When you hurt, that's all you know. It leaves no room to enjoy life. Pain turns people inward and distorts their perceptions.

Imagine what it would be like to have a stone in one shoe that you could not remove. With each step, you would feel a jabbing pain. You would hop or walk on tiptoe. You would learn to avoid certain streets or buildings that didn't accommodate your altered gait. This may seem a trivial example, but notice how one small stone affects you. No more tennis or bowling. No treadmill or StairMaster. No walking for pleasure. No dancing. You would have to find or hire someone to walk your dog. You would have to admit the extent to which the chronic pain and accompanying physical limitations had changed your life and colored your perception of the world.

The same is true of emotional pain. A wound need not be severe for it to influence your relationships, your emotions, and your ability to enjoy a social life. In my clinical experience with patients I've found that many people harbor emotional stones that are far larger than would fit in a shoe.

People don't show us their pain; in fact, they try to hide it. What we see is their behavior. When a person's behavior is out of bounds, we can easily and understandably think of him or her as callous or cruel, but their behaviors are often dysfunctional adaptations to their psychological or emotional pain. More often than not, the people who have hurt us have acted out of their own insecurity and reflexive sense of defensiveness.

One way that I've learned to approach forgiveness is to picture people who frustrate or anger me by thinking of them as they were when they were babies, totally open, vulnerable, trusting, wanting to laugh and be loved. "I wonder what Sylvia was like as a baby. *What the hell happened!?* How much pain must she have endured to become so broken and downright mean?" or some such thing.

I fully realize that, relatively speaking, I've had it easy. In some situations I've confronted clinically, I have to admit that I'd be hard-pressed to find my way to forgiveness.

One family's story in particular sticks in my mind.

The Personal Economics of Pain

Lynne Halamish, the grief counselor in Israel, told me about an extraordinary case that provides lessons for all of us about how finding a way to forgive even people who have done us grievous wrongs is in our own self-interest.

Avi was a 45-year-old man when his father, Simon, was dying of lung cancer that had spread to his spine. Their history had been full of pain and heartache.

Simon had divorced his first wife while his son was still in the womb. Avi grew up with his mother in a small Israeli village. Although people knew that Simon could be mean-spirited, he owned a large grocery store and was active in local politics, so his word held a lot of weight. Avi, particularly as a young boy, craved his father's attention and did everything he could think of to elicit even the slightest sign of approval. Every effort was rebuffed, often publicly. Simon systematically ignored or intentionally tripped up Avi at every turn. As if this wasn't painful enough, Simon remarried and had two children with his second wife. They received Simon's attention, while Avi was completely shut out from his father's life.

Lynne was called in a week after Simon had suddenly lost control of his lower body, becoming all but paralyzed over a period of 18 hours. During the course of urgently evaluating his sudden dramatic weakness, the doctors found that the lung cancer had damaged his spinal cord.

As Lynne spoke with Simon about his illness and life, she gradually became aware that he had an ex-wife and another son. When she realized this, she tried to meet with Avi, who at first refused. She did meet with his mother and in the process learned more about their family and Avi's troubled relationship with his father. Together, Lynne and Avi's mother developed a plan in which his mother asked Avi to meet with Lynne, "for my sake."

When Lynne finally did meet Avi, they sparred for the first few minutes, but once he realized she could take his verbal barbs—and give back in kind—he warmed up. They quickly established a rapport and talked about his mother and their family life. Avi was almost casual in saying that he hated his father.

Undeterred, Lynne introduced the notion of saying the Four Things. When she told Avi that she thought it would be valuable for him to say them to his father, he stared at her and became beet red. "Are you crazy?" he said. "I should ask forgiveness from *him!* Do you have any idea what hell he put me through? There is no way in hell I could forgive the son-of-a-bitch. I can't do it."

Lynne pressed Avi. It is difficult to forgive someone, but difficult is not impossible. We can *decide* to forgive someone. First and foremost, forgiveness is an act of volition and will.

Avi yelled at her: "This isn't about decisions. I feel only hatred for him. Do you think for a minute that I could feel forgiveness after all he's done?"

The forgiveness that the Four Things requests, however, has nothing to do with *feeling* one way or another. Avi could hate his father; you might hate someone, too. And Avi could admit that in so many words. What was necessary for Avi was to say "I forgive you" to his father so he wouldn't have to carry around the weight of his unresolved relationship with his father after his father died.

It is wrong to think that people need to *feel* forgiveness in order to *give* forgiveness. Forgiveness is actually about emotional economics. It's about a one-time cost that you pay to clear up years of compounded emotional pain. It's like taking a one-time loss in financial investments. Refusing to forgive means accepting the cost of the hurts inflicted on you compounded a thousand times. And it means carrying them forever as they accrue in negative emotional energy.

Refusing to forgive is a decision to remain in debt. If I give you 10 dollars and you don't pay it back, I can carry the debt and be reminded of it every month and every time I see you, or I can take on the cost by forgiving that debt once and for all. Emotional debts are like this. Avi had already paid enough for the things Simon had done to him. He didn't need to keep on paying for the rest of his life.

Avi was still unconvinced, but he recognized that he had wasted enough time allowing his feelings to rule his life. It was time for him to make a cold, calculated decision that would release him from the bondage of hatred toward his father. Even if his father didn't deserve forgiveness, Avi *did*. His father was going to die. Avi was the one who would carry the animosity and resentment in the years to come. He had carried them long enough.

A Clean Slate

Avi grudgingly decided to forgive Simon for the mean, rotten things he had done and said when Avi was a kid. But what was *he*, Avi, supposed to ask forgiveness for?

Lynne asked Avi why he thought Simon had been so cruel.

"Because he is a vile *%$#^&*! That's why," said Avi.

When Lynne admitted that that theory was as good as any, Avi laughed out loud. But why, she asked, when Avi was small, say seven or eight years old, was Simon such a monster to him?

"I always thought it was because I wasn't good enough for him," Avi replied.

Lynne then suggested that Avi apologize to Simon for never having been good enough for him.

Again, Avi nearly convulsed. "What!" he said. "You want me to say I'm sorry that I wasn't good enough to be his son?!"

Lynne told him that wasn't the point. What mattered was getting as clean a slate as possible in his relationship to his father before he died. Time was short.

After considerable discussion, Avi reluctantly agreed to give it a try. Then he and Lynne came to the fourth thing, I love you. She wasn't sure what was going to happen when she broached this with Avi, but she had been able to use the Four Things so successfully with so many other clients, she wasn't willing to skip it. But when she told Avi to say "I love you," to Simon, she thought he was going to walk out on her. "I tell you I hate this man and you tell me to cuddle with him?" he said. "What is it with you?"

Lynne acknowledged that "I love you" would not be the easiest three words for Avi to say to his father, but she also pointed out that if his need for his father's love wasn't so strong, the lack of it wouldn't be causing Avi so much pain. Lynne told Avi to try to connect with the good father he had never had and always wished for, and to tell *that* father, the one he had always wanted, that he loved him.

Lynne knew she was pushing Avi to the edge, but she also knew they were pressed for time. She had seen Simon that morning and wasn't sure that he'd make it through the week. He looked withered and gray and would frequently drift off to sleep. In that, there was one advantage. As Simon physically deteriorated, his personality had changed, startlingly, for the better. Avi's father had turned into an almost sweet guy for the first time in his life. The people who came to visit him commented that he seemed to have mellowed and softened.

When Lynne had finished talking about saying the Four Things, Avi said, "The only thing I'm looking forward to saying to this man is good-bye." Knowing that their time was up, he looked her in the eye and asked with his ironic humor, "Are we finished with the hard part yet?"

"Not quite," she told him. "Your father is very, very sick, so you need to say the Four Things today."

Avi shook his head with a rueful smile—but that evening, he entered his father's room.

Avi stopped by to see Lynne the next day. He was in notably good humor, and much lighter than when they'd met earlier.

"Well," he said. "I did as you suggested. I asked my father to forgive me and said I was sorry for never having been able to measure up in his eyes. Then I said that I forgave him for being so cold and distant. And, I gotta tell you, after I said these things, it felt like a weight had been lifted from my chest. But when it came time to say 'I love you,' I wasn't able to say it as a statement, so I spoke the words as a question. He was lying in his bed and I leaned my head to the side and bent towards him, trying to see the man I had wanted to love me and be my father. 'I love you?' I said. And this man, who was my father in biology only, looked up and his eyes got wet and red and he hugged me. It was the first time that I can remember him even touching me. And then he said, 'I love you, too.'"

Lynne asked Avi if he'd said "Thank you" and he said that yes, he had thanked his father for giving him life. Anything else? she wondered. He looked bewildered. "What else could I possibly thank him for?" How about for the hug? she said. Avi just smiled, nodded his head, and laughed. He didn't say anything, but got up from his chair, came over, and hugged her. "Thank *you*," he said to her before he left the clinic.

Avi's good-bye to Simon came a few weeks later when his father was unconscious (he was a tough old man and managed to stay alive longer than anyone could have predicted). But that was not the last Lynne heard from Avi. He called her several months after Simon's death to say that the Four Things had changed his whole life. In forgiving his father he found he'd become forgiving toward his children, his wife, and himself. And, he told her, he had realized that before he had managed to forgive Simon, he had been becoming the worst parts of his father to his own children.

Without knowing it, Avi had been perpetuating many of the traits—such as being quick to judge, overly critical, and rigid in his ways—that he despised in Simon. Avi's pain at the repeated wounds inflicted by his father's unkind words and willful neglect caused him to confine his feelings in a steel-tight, protective cage. He had kept them locked inside, afraid that they would escape as rage and wound the people closest to him, as he had been wounded.

Courage to Open a Locked Heart

As Avi forced himself to speak words of forgiveness and love to his father, a remarkable thing occurred; his own heart heard them, too. He felt the rage inside him dissolve. Suddenly, he sensed that he could feel deeply without worrying that he would lose control. He felt an exhilarating rush of well-being.

Lynne's savvy and therapeutic rapport helped Avi, but it took remarkable courage for Avi to take a chance, to open up and to forgive Simon. As deep and justified as his anger was, Avi was willing to look inward and consider that raging at his father might not be his only option—nor the best response from the perspective of his own happiness and his relationships with his wife and children. He opened to the possibility of healing. He had thought that the wounds his father had inflicted were all old, but in completing his relationship with Simon, Avi discovered that the damage had been ongoing. He had long been trapped in an emotionally toxic shell that he had made and only he could break. In the warm flood of well-being that accompanied saying the Four Things with his father Avi realized that enlightened self-interest is at the core of the wisdom of forgiveness.

If you feel challenged by the example Avi set, you're not alone. I myself am hot-blooded by temperament. I grew up reflexively raging at anyone who hurt me and holding a grudge. Righteous indignation can be seductive, and even addictive, but unresolved anger is toxic to your happiness and your relationships. Stories of people like Avi have challenged me over the years to let go of these self-destructive emotions. Opening my heart is a daily practice. It is not easy, but it is much more rewarding and healthy than carrying grudges.

"But what if I fail?" people ask. As long as you are clear and positive in your intentions, you have nothing to fear, and nothing to lose. Even if you forgive someone and he or she reacts in an utterly irrational way, you will discover that your good-faith efforts help *you* feel better about the relationship. *You* will be able to let go of negative feelings and feel at peace with yourself. By practicing forgiveness, you can milk the poison out of even the most venomous relationship.

CHAPTER EIGHT

Extreme Acts of Forgiveness

Sometimes extending forgiveness can be incredibly hard. What can we do when someone we once trusted wounds us so deeply that forgiveness seems inconceivable?

This is not a theoretical question. In my years practicing in hospital emergency departments, I saw many things that would have been unthinkable if they hadn't actually occurred. I've seen the results of physical abuse of infants and young children, including beating and scalding, that have left painful, permanent physical scars. I've seen children, even babies, who have been sexually molested by relatives or family friends. Treating these children, I was doubly grieved by knowing that in the future these victims typically find it hard to form intimate, loving, and lasting relationships.

On the other hand, in my work in hospice and palliative care, I've met people who, as adults, have been forced to

confront these difficult issues and have discovered in themselves courage and resilience that is awe inspiring. When a
mother or father is becoming increasingly frail and approaching the end of her or his life, the question for the
adult child who was abused becomes, "How can I reach
some satisfactory sense of completion?"

Sometimes, the abused person asks, "Why should I
bother?"

It's a good question. Distance and disdain are legitimate
options, but completing the relationship—including being
willing to extend forgiveness—is the surest way to dissolve
old scars. This forgiveness is not about accepting or excus-
ing the abuse. It is not altruism. You may be entirely justified in hating the person who abused you, but hate keeps
you chained to the person you despise.

Some of the abuse I've seen and the stories I have heard
in the course of my practice have made forgiveness seem
unattainable. Yet people like Maeve Heaton remind me
that forgiveness is always possible—and necessary if people
want to break free of the past and become healthy and
whole.

"It Hasn't Always Been Easy"

Maeve told me her story of forgiveness when she had come
to see her father, Patrick, an 83-year-old widower, who had
retired to Montana from Chicago and didn't have long to
live. He was in a Missoula nursing home, dying of repeated
strokes and spreading prostate cancer. The cancer had

metastasized to his bones. The pain and the radiation treatments needed to control it were sapping his strength. He was comfortable, but had lost interest in eating and was gradually losing weight.

I noticed when I was in his room that Maeve seemed reserved, maybe even a bit aloof, although she was attentive and kind with her father. He was mostly silent in her presence. They rarely spoke or made eye contact. I thought this odd, since Maeve had flown to Missoula all the way from Pittsburgh, where she worked as a stock market analyst, to spend time with her father during his final days.

On my next visit to the nursing home two days later, Maeve was sitting quietly in her father's room while he slept. I asked her if she would like to talk over a cup of coffee. She said she would and we walked to a private corner of the day room. Maeve had the look of a successful, independent professional: a carefully coiffed, poised woman in her midforties in a tailored gray suit. "It was good of you to come all the way from Pittsburgh to be with your dad," I said.

She looked me in the eye. "Well," she said. "He's my father and it's my responsibility." She sighed, adding, "God knows, it hasn't always been easy being his daughter."

I recognized Maeve's comment as a tentative invitation, a way of her letting me know there was a story there to tell and finding out whether I was willing to hear more. I said, "I only met your father within the past few weeks so I don't have a good sense of what he was like in his earlier life. In what ways has it been hard to be Patrick's daughter?"

"It's a small miracle I'm here at all," she answered. "I never thought I would be able to forgive my father." She paused, as if inwardly firming her resolve, before pouring out her story.

Maeve had been Daddy's little girl. Her earliest memory had been playing hide and seek with him. Each night he, not her mother, had read her bedtime stories. He was the parent she ran to when she hurt herself.

Patrick came from a strict Irish Catholic family in Chicago. He was an altar boy who had once considered the priesthood. His father was an alcoholic, and, by the time Patrick was a young man, he was drinking more than was good for him. Maeve suspected he had been sexually molested as a boy, perhaps in his church.

He started abusing her when she was nine. He would come into the bathroom when she was showering and have her perform oral sex on him. "He told me," said Maeve, "that it was 'our special love' and 'our special time.' He told me that it was our secret and that I mustn't tell anyone about it."

Not surprisingly, Maeve coped by "checking out," dissociating her awareness from her body. It was as if she were outside herself, watching it happen.

Except at those times, her father acted toward her as he always had. He was stern and attentive, with high expectations for her grades and behavior. He showed real interest in her school projects and after-school activities. At the time, Maeve was too young to know what to think. Mostly she suppressed any thought of those "special times," and, of course, her father never mentioned them. They were like a recurring bad dream, discontinuous from waking life.

Her father stopped abusing her at 13, but the damage

had been done. She became a sullen withdrawn teenager and, at 15, swallowed an overdose of Tylenol and was hospitalized. She couldn't explain to the consulting psychologist why she had tried to end her life. "I told them I felt stupid and promised not to try to hurt myself again. They would have locked me in a psychiatric unit unless I agreed to see a psychologist twice a week."

Maeve's parents were at a loss to explain her actions—at least her mother was. She kept invoking "hormones," as if her daughter had been poisoned by puberty.

"People assumed I was having a typical adolescent crisis," Maeve said. "Three weeks after I took the Tylenol, I ran away." Maeve looked off into the distance. "I won't say what happened during that time, but, eventually, I showed up at the door of my favorite aunt and uncle, Margaret and Phil. They welcomed me with open arms. When they asked me why I ran away, I kept saying, 'I'm just not happy there, please don't send me back!'"

Maeve's parents agreed that she could finish the school year in Pittsburgh on the condition that she continued in counseling.

Time passed and Maeve became less withdrawn; her school performance improved. She grew increasingly close to Aunt Margaret, her father's sister. Finally, she confided to her aunt about those "special times."

A stunned and outraged Margaret flew to Chicago and confronted her brother. At first he denied everything, but when Margaret threatened to report him to the legal authorities, he confessed, hid his face in shame, and agreed to seek professional help.

"He immediately quit drinking," Maeve recalled. "He started seeing a counselor and began attending group therapy with Catholic men who had been abusers."

Over the next few years, Maeve didn't see her father at all. She thrived in Margaret and Phil's home. She graduated high school with honors and began college at the University of Pennsylvania with her parents paying tuition. She went on to Wharton and earned an MBA.

Shortly before her mother's death, she made contact with her father. She knew it had been her mother's deepest wish. In their first contact in more than 10 years, Patrick's counselor was present. Her father tearfully confessed the inexcusable things he had done to her. He told her how wrong he was and how sorry he felt.

I asked Maeve if her father had explicitly asked her to forgive him.

"He said he didn't feel worthy to ask my forgiveness. But he said he hoped in time I could find a way to forgive him."

"Were you able to?"

"Yes, over time. What he did was wrong. It was a sick thing to do. But I think he was sick. He'd been poisoned by his upbringing and by alcohol. I could forgive him, but I couldn't absolve him. He did what he did. I don't think the priests could absolve him either."

I asked Maeve what she thought had made it possible for her to forgive her father.

"For one thing, my own counseling. My therapist helped me to sort out what was real and right and normal from what was my own damaged sense of reality. I couldn't have done any of it without that sort of professional help."

"Second, it was important that my father admitted what he had done and reached out to me. If he hadn't, I don't think I could have ever forgiven him. I'm not sure I would have ever spoken to him again. If he hadn't apologized and been so obviously ashamed, it would have diminished him even further in my eyes."

"And so you're here now."

She sighed and smiled wanly. "Yes, I'm here. I don't hate him. I think he hated himself for what he did."

I asked Maeve how she felt now that her father was dying.

"I'm mostly sad," she said. "He is still my father. Even with the things he did, part of me loves him. It took me a long while to come to some peace with it. I'm not willing to feel bad about myself. No life is perfect. I think about babies who are born in refugee camps and will likely live within barbed-wire fences their whole lives. I think of children born into wars, who know only horror and die by age ten. What can I say? I'm grateful for being alive."

Patrick died two days later and Maeve sought me out to say good-bye before she flew back East.

"I must say," I told her, "I think it's amazing that you were able to forgive your dad. You're an inspiration to all of us."

"Therapy taught me that people can recover," she said. "It convinced me that *I* could recover. And I did."

Recovery from serious illness, mental or physical, takes determination. It also takes time, sometimes lots of it. Do what you can today, and leave what you can't for tomorrow. Maeve said it perfectly, "The most important thing I did was to decide and declare that I was going to become whole!"

An Act of Affirmation

Maeve's story is one of hope, wisdom, and courage. When her teenage cries for help went unheard, she escaped and sought safety with her aunt and uncle. What a life-affirming thing to do! She accepted help—something people who have been abused often lack the trust to do.

Like most people who survive sexual abuse as a child and eventually heal, Maeve worked hard in formal therapy. This, too, takes courage. If you're deeply wounded, you may think you can do it alone, and maybe you can, but what will that prove? Why not seek a qualified compassionate counselor and make the passage to healing easier on yourself?

It's worth repeating that forgiveness is not about the other person; it's about you. Whether or not the person who abused you benefits from your forgiveness is not the issue. The issue is the quality of *your* life. Forgiveness is an act of affirmation on your part. It is a way of letting go of old wounds that weigh you down.

Completing a seriously wounded primary relationship is part of emotional self-care, whether or not the relationship continues. Relationships involve two people, and you can only take care of your part.

Maeve chose and was able to reestablish a relationship with her father. In reaching out to her father in the careful, tentative way she did, she was practicing self-care. His willingness to admit and apologize for his misdeeds made a renewed relationship possible. Some adult daughters in similar situations have tried to talk with their fathers only to have them steadfastly deny ever doing anything of the sort. It's impossible for them to feel that anything was resolved. But in making a good-faith effort they have completed their side of the relationship. They know they have done all they could and are free of a set of "should haves," "could haves," and "what ifs" that might have nagged at them forever.

CHAPTER NINE

Forgiving Yourself

One of the most important lessons I have learned over the years from people who were dying is the wisdom of self-forgiveness. This single lesson can boost our sense of self-worth, transforming our lives.

Susan Armstrong, a wife and mother dying of ALS— amyotrophic lateral sclerosis or Lou Gehrig's disease— wrestled with inner doubts and a sense of guilt about her diagnosis. For the first six months of her illness, she was unable to find any peace within herself and she felt guilty for not being at peace.

The Search for Emotional Peace

When I sat down with Richard Armstrong to talk about his late wife, he told me that although the Four Things are mostly about a person's relationship with others in his or her life, Susan had needed to say and feel them within herself.

"We married in our midthirties," he explained. "I know that somehow Susan grew up not feeling good about herself, but I never really understood why she felt the way she did. It was ironic. For instance, she was absolutely gorgeous, but we hardly have any pictures of her. She was self-conscious and, as I learned in our first years of marriage, not really at peace with herself."

Everyone who met Susan saw a vibrant 42-year-old woman who seemed calm and self-possessed, even in the face of her scary diagnosis. Like many shy or self-conscious people, Susan had learned to show a confident face to the world. Strong social skills enabled her to function effectively at work and maintain satisfying friendships.

She and Richard were actively involved in their community. They had met at a Special Olympics fundraiser and discovered they both loved sailing and skiing. They soon became good friends, then best friends and soul mates. They were married within the year. The joy of their marriage redoubled when their daughter, Allison, was born.

Susan was no stranger to illness and death. When she was 14, her mother had died. When it happened, it was a shock. Yet, no one talked to her about it at the time. Richard explained, "I asked her about her mother's death. Sue said she knew her mom was very sick and in pain, but there wasn't a lot of discussion about the illness, before or afterwards." Susan told Richard that she felt abandoned in her grief after her mother died. She couldn't talk to her father or her aunts and uncles about how sad she was that her mother was gone.

Susan also knew from firsthand experience that dying does not have to be hidden—and that even when dying is hard, it doesn't have to be horrible. She had done volunteer work, offering massage to patients with a hospice and an AIDS foundation. She had helped comfort many patients with cancer or AIDS in their dying.

"Susan was simply the best person I have ever met," Richard said, "and the most loved. But she just never felt to herself like the person that everybody loved. There's so much complexity to her history and to the person Susan was that I never did figure it all out. Maybe if we had had another forty years—" His voice cracked and he paused. "About a year and a half after her mom died, her father remarried and his new wife also had three kids, so they became the 'Brady Bunch.' I think there was a lot of love in her family, but there was also a lack of communication and difficulty relating to each other."

When Allison was born, Susan "retired" from her massage practice to be a full-time mom. She had never attended college, which Richard felt was a source of personal regret and low self-confidence. Ironically, six weeks before her symptoms began she had finally enrolled at the university. That fall, with Allison six and well established at school, Susan had finally embarked on a long-range plan to earn a BS in biology and go on to graduate school in physical therapy.

Honoring and tending the physical body, her own and others, were central for Susan. She cooked and served fresh, mostly organic foods to her family. She never smoked. She stretched and meditated every day, and ran six to ten miles at least four times a week.

In October of 2000 she noticed her running stride was off. At first she thought it was her shoes, but within a week it was clearly worse. A neurologist at the University of California at San Francisco ordered a series of tests. "He thought it was probably MS," said Richard, "but said we should wait and see. We didn't have to wait long. The symptoms rapidly progressed, and two months later he diagnosed ALS. Two months after that, she needed a cane and then a walker. Every doctor we saw remarked about the peculiar, alarming rate of progression.

"We read everything we could. I was on the Internet for hours on end and called and faxed records to specialists around the country. There was really nothing to be done that wasn't available and being offered where we were.

"Susan did her best to absorb the bad news and maintain a good attitude. She was a trooper in adapting to the physical limitations, but it all moved too fast. She didn't just adjust bravely. She fought like hell while things were being taken away from her faster than she could ever fully adapt to. She had what we came to call trailing adaptation. In late spring, a month or two before she died, she said, 'March wasn't that bad now that I can look back on it. I would go back to that.'

"But, in fact, she was never happy with March. She wanted to accept her illness and adapt in a psychologically healthy way, but, in fact, she was furious. I can't tell you how many copies of *Tuesdays with Morrie* we were given.

There was a catchphrase that she used to express her frustration, 'I'm not Morrie, Goddamn it!' she said. 'No one's going to write a book about how I handled this philosophically.' She was a realist, dealing with it as best she could—but fighting with dealing with it every day."

No illness affects two people in exactly the same way. Richard explained the pattern of symptoms and pace of progression of Susan's ALS. She had some symptoms that aren't talked about much in ALS literature. ALS isn't supposed to be painful, but Susan was plagued with back pain. It was worse at night because after the first few months, she couldn't turn herself in bed. Richard slept in short bursts in order to turn her. The usual medications just made Susan groggy. She preferred the pain. As bad as it was, physical pain was not her main problem. Her anger, which she turned inward, was.

Richard said that during the early months of the illness Susan was most angry at feeling that the things that made her "Susan" were being aggressively taken away from her. She couldn't work, run, or do housework. She couldn't cook for her daughter or even brush her hair. She began to feel like a bad mother.

Richard explained that Susan's real torment in those months after the diagnosis was self-imposed. She struggled with questions of what she had done to bring this on herself. She wouldn't talk about it. "A few times early on when she had mentioned feeling this way, I couldn't stop myself from reflexively reassuring her," said Richard. "It was probably the wrong thing to do, but how was I supposed to respond? I mean, we had both read all the articles. The cause of ALS is not known. She was in perfect health, had never knowingly exposed herself to any toxins. It just didn't make sense. But it wasn't a rational concern, at least not in the medical sense."

Many of my patients have expressed similar sentiments. It's an interesting quirk of human psychology. We know that death awaits us all. Furthermore, we know—either because we have read about or personally known young people who died—that sometimes people contract lethal illnesses for no apparent reason. Yet when illness strikes, it is natural for people to ask, "Why me?"

Richard's memories spoke volumes about his own anguish at the existential maze in which Susan was trapped. Few people are as selfless and giving as Susan Armstrong.

"It is terribly hard to hear that someone you love and know is pure of heart is suffering from self-doubt and guilt," I said.

My comment struck a chord. "Absolutely!" he said. "The only thing I could ever say that made any impact was to point to various children we know who have had bad things happen, from birth defects, to mental retardation, to a brain tumor. I would say, 'What did those kids do to deserve that?'"

Reading Your Biography

As people come to the end of life, it is so common to have at least a few regrets. People wonder what sort of person they have been. Inevitably there will be things we wish we had a chance to do over, this time "getting it right." There are things that we've said that we will wish we could take back.

When you think of it, how could it be otherwise? Nobody comes to the end of life perfect, any more than we could be perfect throughout our lives. We don't have to give up striving to do things well and set things right to acknowledge that we are, after all, just human. The fact is, we will die imperfect. Sad but true. That's not a failing on any of our parts. Imperfection is an inescapable part of being human.

In working with people who are living with an illness that will likely shorten their lives, I sometimes ask them to conceptualize their life as a long, rich novel. I ask them, "If you were reading this novel and you knew that there was just a chapter or perhaps two left, how would you hope to see it end? Let's assume that as the reader, you were able to see the difficult circumstances that the main character was dealing with and you knew his or her motives were good. You could see that some things had not worked out the way he or she had wanted throughout life. How would you feel toward the protagonist? Wouldn't you feel some degree of mercy?"

I've yet to have someone say no. So I ask, "Can you extend to yourself the same mercy that you would have to the protagonist in this story?"

In one sense, they—and you—are not just the reader, but also the author of this story. We are all at least coauthors of our own life stories. We don't set up the circumstances and can't control the external events. We can only write our part in the story as well as we can. But it will never be perfect. We will never write the perfect story or the perfect biography. It wouldn't be believable if we could.

What we can do, from this moment forward, is live as authentically as possible. This means removing the mask we use to protect ourselves from the world, and from being truly seen by others. It means encountering others and the world with honesty, without pretense or ulterior motives. The psychological mask and emotional armor we wear to protect ourselves from hurt diminishes the integrity and intensity of our lives. When we are willing to allow others to see us as we are and when we trust our clear, good intentions and reflect them in our words and deeds, we are authentically ourselves. In so doing, we need never have regrets.

Like so many others, Susan asked herself "Why me?" ten thousand times, running through every conceivable reason, physical and metaphysical, in a futile effort to explain the unexplainable. Ultimately, she gave up. Maybe her anger simply lost steam, or she realized that angry or not, life was going on around her. No one can know if Susan fully resolved her anger, but she was able to put it aside. Instead of looking inward, she decided that there were people out there who commanded her attention. She decided to focus outward and invested the last of her life in the people who gave her meaning. In doing so she found renewed meaning and a measure of peace in her remaining life.

Worthy Right Here, Right Now

A piercing lesson we can all take from Susan's story is that none of us need wait to accept ourselves. We are worthy of self-acceptance and of love right now. Even with our imperfections. All of us have the things we wish we hadn't done, even dark secrets that we hide in shame. You may think that other people don't have them, but they do. Yes, you are flawed, you have made many mistakes, some serious. So what? Who hasn't? It only proves you are human. Please forgive yourself and show yourself some love.

Feelings of unworthiness and self-loathing cause untold suffering. They can make people feel alone and unwanted in a roomful of friends. That's why it is so important to get over it—admitting that you are who you are and that's good enough—because until you are able to feel worthy, other people may love you, but you will be unable to believe them, or feel their love. And you deserve to feel their love! You are worthy of love right here, right now. It can—and must—start with loving yourself.

CHAPTER TEN

Living with Uncertainty and Illness

If by chance you are living with an illness, please be kind to yourself. Have mercy! Don't expect to be a perfect patient. You can't be ill perfectly. You are just human. Thankfully, that's good enough.

It is astounding how many people struggling with chronic conditions (such as cancer, heart, lung, or kidney disease, crippling arthritis, or strokes) also suffer from embarrassment or even shame at being sick. We instinctively look for the causes of the traumatic events in our lives. An unintended consequence of our preoccupation with exercise, diet, and healthy lifestyles is that when we become ill, we think we're somehow at fault.

If we learn that someone has cancer, we think, "Well, she is a smoker." If we hear that a coworker was injured in a serious car accident, we ask, "Was he wearing a seat belt?" We explain away other people's misfortune in a futile attempt to protect ourselves from our own fragility and mortality.

When our time comes and sickness or injury forces us to face death, the question for each of us will be, Can we show ourselves the same mercy that we would show to another person who is living through this unwanted, inherently difficult time of life?

"I Am Not a Bad Person"

Often when I sit with people who are dying and struggling with feeling worthless or unworthy, I ask, "What have you really done so wrong? We're here together, there's no one else here with us, tell me the secret. Who have you killed this week? What horrible acts have you committed that make you feel unworthy?"

If they can't convince me of their wretchedness (and no one yet has) I ask, "Now that you know that time may be growing short, can you finally accept the fact that you are indeed worthy and lovable?"

It's poignant to sit with someone who was a smoker and is dying of lung cancer. They feel guilty for having brought misfortune on themselves. I ask them, "Do you think that if you never smoked, you would have lived forever? Really, your main diagnosis is not cancer or heart disease; it's being mortal."

I ask them to engage in a therapeutic exercise. "I want you to look in the mirror and see yourself, fully acknowledging that you have been a smoker for twenty years—and that you would still like a cigarette right now!—and I want you to say, 'I am a good person.'"

That's difficult for many people. Sometimes I suggest a meditative exercise for people struggling with this sense of being unworthy. I teach them to relax, eyes closed, and envision a wheel on the edge of which is written, "I am not a bad person. I am not a bad person."

I say, "Can you use that image and those words when you are alone with your own thoughts, as a way of relaxing and challenging yourself in a loving way to accept your inherent worthiness?" Sometimes people say, "Oh, Doctor, I couldn't do that." They get squeamish, as if it is unseemly to feel that good about themselves.

If they are with me this far, I tell them, "This is just the first step. When you are able to say to yourself, 'I am not a bad person,' I will raise the bar and ask you to imagine the edge of that wheel inscribed with the phrase, 'I am a good person.' There are people around you who love you, who want you to know how deeply they love you, but unless you can feel a sense of your own inherent worthiness, you will not be able to feel how much love there is for you."

Accepting Your Humanity

If you are stuck in guilt about being ill and unworthy of love, you won't be able to experience the acceptance others have for you. You will never be able to understand or feel how important and valued you are in their eyes. That is real suffering: to feel isolated, unworthy, and alone in the midst of those who do love you. You need not let that happen because you *are* worthy. Our imperfection is a sign of our humanity. It makes us real.

Anyone living with serious, debilitating conditions has something to teach all of us, whether we're ill or not. Being ill and physically dependent has nothing to do with dignity. Physical frailty is not a sign of personal weakness or moral insufficiency. It is simply and inevitably part of all of us. We would never consider the complete physical dependence and utter incontinence of an infant to be in any way undignified. It is simply part of being an infant.

Think of how you feel toward infants who depend on their families or others for every physical need. We love them. We pamper them; we couldn't do otherwise. *If we ignored them, we would be less than human.* I mean this literally. There is a body of research on the biology of altruism that makes a strong case that humans possess an innate drive to care for others. We are hard-wired to clean, feed, and nurture babies. People hum, coo, and sing to infants not only to comfort them, but evoke a smile.

Now ask yourself, Will those babies be less deserving of loving care and attention when they are seriously ill, frail, elderly, and once again physically dependent? Even when they are once again incontinent, as virtually all human beings will once again be? Would we not bathe and cleanse and hold and nurture them as others once did when they were infants?

As adults we tend to think that our accomplishments and standing in society somehow shield us from the supposed indignity of physical dependence. *This is an illusion.*

In an emergency room the vulnerability and fragility of our bodies are inescapable, but so is our fundamental commonality. A person doesn't have to be dying to be utterly dependent and in need of care. I once cared for a powerful politician who was half-carried into the ER, drenched in sweat and doubled over in pain caused by the kidney stone he was trying to pass. And I recall a wealthy, prim middle-aged woman who came in by ambulance, severely dehydrated from uncontrollable vomiting and diarrhea due to stomach flu. In such inherently ungraceful circumstances, dignity resides in wise recognition of one's predicament and a gracious acceptance of help from others.

Our Inherent Dignity

If you are reading this when you are dependent on others for care—even dressing, eating, bathing, and toileting—please have mercy for yourself. Don't worry about being undignified. Your dignity is intact.

People are inherently dignified. The notion that sickness or disability is somehow undignified is the source of endless, unnecessary suffering. It's heartbreaking to meet people who are embarrassed simply because they're ill or need help from others. My father was the person who showed me this cultural trap. If we believe health and independence are absolute virtues, illness and physical dependence can feel like personal failures or even vices. In 1980, I was driving Dad home after a radiation treatment he received for his pancreatic cancer.

He sat next to me in the front seat of his station wagon as I took a scenic route along the Jersey Shore, heading to the home where I grew up. At a stoplight I looked over at him and let my gaze linger a moment. Before the cancer, Dad had been a heavy-set man. Baking was his only hobby and eating his main passion. Now his appetite and energy were all but gone. He had lost his zest for life. He appeared deflated, as though the wind had been knocked out of him. The bones of his face were prominent—his skeleton asserting itself.

We knew that treatment couldn't cure him, but hoped it might buy him some time. I knew that time was precious and wanted to savor every minute we had. My mom wasn't expecting us for at least another hour, so I asked Dad if he wanted to get a cup of coffee or a hot dog at a favorite lunch place owned by a friend of his.

He said, "No, I don't think so." When I persisted, he said, "I don't look so good. I look sick and I think I smell bad, sicklike, too." I hid my tears from him as I drove, but I will never forget the unfairness of my father feeling embarrassed simply for being ill!

Americans have an exaggerated notion of the importance of being independent and self-sufficient—both of which can be virtues. At some point, however, it is entirely appropriate to rely on others. It is important to recognize your need for others when you're ill. To do otherwise is unhealthy, not just physically, but also emotionally. I have seen people who refuse to do so: the hard-charging executive who refuses to admit that his heart condition is forcing him to slow down; the frail, forgetful 85-year-old woman who refuses to stop driving. At some point it becomes just plain unnatural.

Some self-help books have made "codependence" into a pathologic diagnosis. Certainly, unhealthy relationships do exist that reinforce people's addictions and unhealthy patterns of behavior. That's not what we're talking about here. It is wholly natural, normal, and necessary for human beings to depend on one another. Wholesome codependence is part of loving relationships between spouses, parents, and children and close friends.

Living in a Human Community

Human beings are innately social animals. It is natural for people to live in community with one another—rather than merely in proximity to one another. Living in community means acknowledging our innate interdependence and accepting a level of mutual responsibility for one another. The most concrete example of this fact is the government's pledge to care for its citizens with Social Security. But the principle of shared responsibility is evident in a thousand expectations and norms of behavior not only within the body politic, but also in the civic communities of towns and neighborhoods and in workplaces, social clubs, and congregations. It is a mark of a healthy community that members care for one another during periods of stress and need, and can be counted on to do so.

In part, society discharges its collective responsibility to its members who are ill by training and paying professional caregivers—doctors, nurses, social workers, therapists, and aides. But all of us retain some direct responsibilities as well. In our daily lives, this may mean simply checking in with a person who we see regularly in our apartment building, neighborhood, office, congregation, or corner store, and who we notice is getting weaker with each passing day. If it is a sibling, parent, or close friend who is seriously ill, fulfilling our responsibilities may well require juggling other responsibilities and schedules and showing up for however long and however often we're needed.

There is another, equally important aspect to mutual responsibility. Allowing others to support and care for us when we're ill is also essential to the well-being of our communities. Indeed, refusing to be cared for erodes the living bonds that form a community. A person who is ill (physically or with an emotional illness like depression) and isolates himself because he doesn't want to bother his family and friends is destined to wind up in dire straits that could have been prevented. How will your family feel when they find you on the floor of your home, or when they find out that you died alone and in pain? You will not have saved them distress. The truth is *we already are a burden to our family and friends.* There is no way to avoid it—and it would be unhealthy to try. The best we can do is to minimize the burden we are to others. Being as cooperative as possible when it is our turn to receive care is the responsible, socially correct, and healthy thing to do.

Burden and Value of Caregiving

Caregiving is a burden and can exact a costly toll, but it also fills an intrinsic need that people feel to love and care for one another. Just as we would be less human if we didn't reflexively respond to an infant in need, we would also be less than who we are if we neglected a dying mother, father, sister, brother, or close friend. I'm not saying this to lay a trip on family members; I'm saying it because it's true. If you are ill and feeling awful because you're a burden to your family, consider this: In important ways, they *need* to care for you.

As hard as it is to accept, if you have been stricken with a debilitating illness or injury, please let yourself be the designated "ill person" in your family or network of friends. Your role is to be cared for. If people ask to care for you, PLEASE LET THEM! The truth is that your family and friends have more at stake in this than you do.

We are all going to die. Accept this lesson from people who have gone before you: When it's your turn, forgive yourself your own mortality. When you are sick or needy in some way, let those around you in. When you fail to do this, you increase the burden on the people closest to you who are going to have to live with the consequences of your refusal, reluctance, or unwillingness to be cared for the rest of *their* lives. If you want to take good care of them, let them take good care of you!

PART THREE

Thank You

*There is more hunger for love and appreciation
in this world than for bread.*

MOTHER TERESA

Introduction

The longer I work in the field of hospice and palliative care, the more I see the practical value of stating the obvious. This is especially true of "Thank you." All of us have a need to express gratitude and to feel appreciated.

People think it's not necessary to express thanks. They say, for example, "She knows how much I appreciate all she has done for me." When I hear that, I reply, "Good, then it'll take no time at all to tell her again."

Working with people who are dying has taught me that the people who are supposed to know how much they're appreciated often don't. At the end of life, people often have a particular need to hear that their actions have made a difference, that they have made a contribution.

Why wait to tell them that they're appreciated? It costs nothing to state the obvious—and no mumbling allowed. Here are some examples of how you can broach the subject:

"Dad, I can never thank you enough for all you have done for me and all you have given me over the years." "Mom, you have always been there for me. You gave me life and you were my best friend. Thank you with all my heart." To a spouse or life partner: "Thank you for all your love. Thank you for putting up with me!"

This is one place where being redundant never hurts.

It's not only important to express gratitude—it's also important to be able to receive it, take it in, and feel appreciated. Receiving thanks is not why we do things for others. Mostly we are motivated by responsibility, concern, camaraderie, appreciation, and love. But there is a healthy satisfaction in being able to accept a heartfelt "thank you."

When we are truly able to accept that kind of thank-you, a wonderful sense of resolution can occur. We feel recognized and accepted, and we complete the emotional transaction that began when we were thoughtful, considerate, or generous.

Saying thank you can be a solid, practical first step toward completing an important relationship. General thanks "for being you" are fine for a friend, sibling, or lover, or a "thank you for giving me life" to a parent. But once you get started, I encourage you to be as specific as possible. The inverse of taking things for granted is to be mindful—and thankful for—small kindnesses. Our relationships, and indeed our lives, can too easily become habitual, insulating us from experiencing what a miracle it is to be alive, and how much is given to us each moment.

Stephen Levine put this beautifully in his book *A Year to*

Live, "We cannot feign gratitude any more than we can pretend forgiveness. Gratitude is a way of seeing, of being. It is a response of our innate wisdom to our accumulated confusion. It is the luminous ground on which we plant our temporary feet."

CHAPTER ELEVEN

Practicing Gratitude

Meister Eckhart, a fourteenth-century Christian theologian and mystic wrote, "If the only prayer you say in your whole life is 'thank you,' that would suffice."

Please take a moment to thank someone you love when he or she smiles at you. The next time you put your child to bed or before you and your spouse retire, try enumerating everything he or she did that day that touched you, that fulfilled his or her responsibilities in your life together, that acknowledged the connection you share.

By paying attention to the details of the ways in which people give to us and show us care and consideration, we become more mindful of our own lives. We begin to focus on our own good fortune rather than our problems. If we practice this consistently and diligently, feelings of gratitude can pervade our lives.

Biographies of Joy

In a remarkable small book, *Joy, Inspiration, and Hope*, Jungian psychiatrist Verena Kast talks about helping people create biographies of joy. This technique helps her treat people for depression and counsel people who are approaching the end of life. I have also found this a particularly powerful approach to help people look at their lives in a positive, constructive way, especially when they are struggling with grief over lost loved ones or friends.

"Joy tolerates no isolation," Kast writes. "Joy is the emotion that lets down our guard, for better or worse. Joy opens us up. . . . Joy is the state in which we are least likely to reflect on ourselves. In the moment of delight, we are; there is nothing we have to do . . . when we are joyful, we feel self-confident and accept ourselves, knowing that our existence is not a matter of indifference. To put it the other way around, when we accept ourselves, we are likely to be delighted in and feel accepted by the world, experiencing an affinity with that which transcends us, with other persons, and with the spiritual."

You can begin to create your own biography of joy by thinking back to when you were a small child. How did joy feel in your body? Are you someone who tended to giggle or sing when you felt joyful? As you grew a bit older, what continued to give you joy: Christmas mornings, birthdays, a special family trip? In your teens, what evoked joy? Perhaps you felt joy after a successful piano or dance recital, or when you scored a goal in soccer or football. Perhaps you remember a time you felt especially close to your father or mother, or the first time you fell in love.

What happened to joy in your life? For too many of us, joy has been lost. Perhaps we thought it was self-indulgent or childish. But joy is a legitimate part of life—a necessary, essential part of healthy living.

What gives you joy? Playing with babies or young children? Visiting with friends or family? Art, music, old movies, mystery novels, or comic strips? It's important to bring joy into your life on a regular basis, even if this notion feels self-indulgent. Consider joy as part of your recommended daily dose of essential vitamins. "Vitamin J" is vital to your well-being.

It's interesting that when I ask people in the throes of terminal illness to talk about what elicited joy in their past, a remarkable thing often occurs. Even if they're suffering, as they recall events in their childhood their expression changes: they smile and sometimes laugh aloud.

It is not unusual for people who are terminally ill to experience this state of joy when death is close. Each moment and each human interaction becomes precious. People who are dying don't take things for granted. In the naked honesty and vulnerability that accompanies proximity to death, even seemingly inconsequential interactions—or simply the presence of another person—can be revealed for the miraculous gifts that they are. Gratitude and joy are intimately fused, and practicing gratitude is a sure way to bring joy into our lives.

In the act of saying thank you we expand ourselves. Thanking people in an explicit way is an act of generosity. By naming what we have been given, we remind ourselves of the surfeit of our experiences, of how replete we are. We invest attention in what we have, rather than what we lack. In most cases, we realize that we have what we need. We begin to recognize how much we've been given.

People at the end of life can seem to lose themselves in the past. They feel drawn as if by gravity to the density and richness of their accumulated life experience. They often express intense gratitude about their lives and for the people they have known. An old French proverb says, "Gratitude is the heart's memory." In gratitude we celebrate who we are to one another and the ways in which our lives have been shaped and moved by each other.

People who are dying seem to grasp the abundance of their life experience. Even as life is slipping away, even as they face ultimate loss, people can feel filled with grace and love. This aspect of dying—this actual, attainable sense of completion and deep peace—is especially common to people who have family support that includes humane, loving palliative care.

I had my own experience with the power of gratitude and the transformation that catalyzes at the end of life. I was personally given the gift of gratitude in a way that I'll never forget.

A Lucky Man

When I met Ernesto, he was dying from colon cancer. As the hospice medical director at the time, I usually saw patients if there were problems with which their own physi-

cian or my hospice nurse colleagues wanted help. In
Ernesto's case, the team wanted me to make regular visits
because I spoke more Spanish than the rest of them.

During my residency training and practice in Fresno,
many of my patients were from Mexico and only spoke
Spanish, so I had had to learn enough to take medical histo-
ries and perform physicals. And I wanted to talk with them!
My take on doctoring has always been that if you can't
kibitz with your patients, what's the point? During my residency I grew to have a special fondness for Mexico and its
people, and today I visit the country whenever I can.

Driving out to meet Ernesto for the first time, I wondered if he would have any interest in the emotional aspects
of this time of life, including the Four Things. From treating Hispanic boys and men, I had seen that many have difficulty dealing with what might be called the softer
emotions, and that "machismo" is a male survival trait in
some cultures. Respect is earned by tolerating risk and
pain, and by appearing invincible. How would machismo
fare in the face of death?

I pulled into the trailer park of a low-income neighborhood in Missoula where Ernesto lived. He was up and
dressed for my first visit. Clearly "the doctor coming" was
an event worthy of preparation. He was just 61 years old,
but looked much older. The skin was loose and bruised beneath his eyes; creases were etched into his forehead and
cheeks. His thin, gray hair was neatly combed and his mus-
tache newly trimmed. He showed no sign of physical distress. He was bright and even animated at times. Meeting
him socially, one might not have thought he was ill. But

that day, looking through clinical eyes, I guessed to myself that he had lost about 30 pounds since the denim shirt he wore had fit.

Ernesto spoke a moderate amount of English; his wife, Julia, a little less. My questions and our subsequent discussions in a mix of Spanish and English were challenging, and, at times, hilarious for us all.

There was a gentility about them both that transcended language, and I was fascinated by their history. Ernesto and Julia had both been born in Mexico and had initially come to California as young children of migrant farm workers. It was a hard life. Migrant children were rarely in the same school more than a month or two. The couple had met and married in Salinas in their teens and traveled together, following available work.

Julia became pregnant a few months later. They were picking cherries in central Oregon when a complication with the pregnancy forced them to stay beyond the harvest. After being hospitalized for a week, the couple was taken in by a local family. With the help of a local church group Ernesto found a job as a janitor with the school district. The pregnancy continued to term and their first daughter was born in Oregon, a United States citizen. They stayed in Oregon for 10 years and both Ernesto and Julia also became citizens.

Following my first visit, Ernesto's cancer progressed rapidly. He seemed to shrink a bit each time I saw him—except for his liver, which was swollen with cancer metastases and tender, its edge felt easily three fingerbreadths below his right ribs. I continued to make visits to their home every couple of weeks. Most of the time Ernesto was in pajamas, lying on the couch when I arrived. I was able to control his pain with morphine tablets, three times a day. I added Prednisone, both to decrease inflammation around his tumors and as a "tonic" to boost his appetite and sense of well-being. During this time, despite continued weight loss, Ernesto had many more good days than bad.

Ernesto, Julia, and I could usually dispatch these physical and pharmacological matters in about 20 minutes and spend the rest of my visit talking. I learned that they had moved to Missoula when their second child was two and Ernesto got a job as a janitor in the local high school. There was no shame in it for him. He took pride in his work and considered himself a lucky man. Both daughters had graduated college, the first two to do so in their extended family. Their eldest was now married with children of her own. Through careful spending and saving they had no debts and had gathered enough in the bank to ensure that Julia would not have to worry about basic bills after Ernesto died.

My contribution to our hospice team's psychosocial care consisted mainly of stating the obvious—I expressed admiration for all that he, and they, had accomplished.

"*Soy un hombre afortunado* [I am a lucky man]," Ernesto often told me. "*Me siento tan agradecido para los regalos de todo el dios* [I feel so grateful for all God's gifts]." He said, "I have always thought so, but I have never realized quite how fortunate I was until now!"

Ernesto and Julia knew their time together was limited. In the same manner in which they had made decisions over the years about what to do with limited money, they carefully chose to invest their time with family. With my encouragement, Ernesto organized the family photo albums. During weekend visits, their daughters and sons-in-law taped Ernesto and Julia talking about the photos: their parents, long dead; their early life together, following the harvests, their daughters as young children; Ernesto as a strong, handsome young man; the journey of their lives from the hills of northern Mexico to Missoula. They were making heirlooms for their grandchildren.

Las Cuatro Cosas

On my last visit, Ernesto was in a hospital bed in the front room of their trailer. The disease had drained nearly all his energy—he could muster only enough breath for a few words at a time—but he was awake, lucid, and not in pain.

He rested half sleeping, but, when I engaged him, his eyes became bright and he found the energy to smile broadly. I briefly examined him, noting that he had breath sounds at the base of his lungs that sounded like Velcro being pulled apart. These were from fluid in the small air sacs in his lungs and had been there the week before. A small pressure sore on his tailbone from extended bed rest was clean with no signs of infection. Neither would cause distress. I asked Julia if he was still able to swallow pills (he was), how much fluid he was drinking each day (just a few cupfuls), and when he had last voided (that morning). We stood by Ernesto's bedside so that he could hear, and, if necessary, disagree with her responses.

Julia and I made no attempt to hide the fact that time was short. I said that although we had plans in place for any emergency, I fully expected that Ernesto would gradually become more and more sleepy, and die quite gently. Julia said their daughters were now visiting daily and taking turns spending nights with Ernesto, helping their father turn in bed, sip some juice, or even use the bedpan, so that she could get some uninterrupted rest. I hadn't met the couple's daughters during my midweek, midday visits, but I understood from Julia, that they were openly affectionate with Ernesto.

I reviewed the Four Things—"*las cuatro cosas*"—and Julia nodded and said that their affairs were in order and there was nothing left unsaid. They had taken my advice and expressed forgiveness and thanks as a family and were secure in their love for one another. Any concerns I had had about machismo inhibiting Ernesto's capacity to complete relationships were clearly unwarranted.

It was not without reluctance that I began to get ready to leave. I knew this was probably the last time that I'd see Ernesto, but I assured them that I'd be checking on them regularly and reminded them that there was always a hospice nurse on call and that the nurse, or they, could get to me within a few minutes if there was a problem. I gathered my notebook, stethoscope, and coat and had my hand on the doorknob, when Ernesto motioned with his hand for me to come back. Julia asked him what he needed, wondering what was wrong, but he just wordlessly motioned again.

In a few steps I was at the bedrails. Instead of speaking,

with his hand in the air, Ernesto again motioned for me to come closer. I leaned down so I could hear whatever it was he wanted to tell me. In a single swift motion he reached his arm around my neck and with surprising strength pulled me toward him and kissed me on the cheek. *"Te amo, Doctor. Gracias, mi amigo,"* he said, before letting me out of his embrace.

I was surprised, to say the least, by Ernesto's display of affection, but not nearly as startled as Julia. I looked up to see her standing motionless, tears in her eyes. "I have never seen him do that. I don't think he ever kissed a man in his whole life," she said. I told him in my broken Spanish how honored I was to know him and that I would never forget him.

Lying on his deathbed, Ernesto appeared not merely peaceful but radiant. In his dying, Ernesto's capacity to experience and express gratitude had expanded, and, paradoxically, he had grown more fully alive. His thanks to me was infused with deep feelings of contentment and composure. He was ready to say good-bye. As a doctor, I felt satisfied that my patient was well during this time of his dying. And, as a man, I was profoundly moved.

CHAPTER TWELVE

The Unexpected Grace
of Reconnection

In some situations, even stating the obvious is not easy. For instance, how do you say thank you to a person who no longer remembers who you are? Alzheimer's disease and similar dementias can rob people of the ability to recognize their family. In the process, those who love the person can feel robbed of the opportunity to complete that relationship. Perhaps the lesson of dementia is to say the Four Things early, and often.

Even with advanced dementia, however, small miracles do happen. Moments of startling clarity can flash like lightning and leave us breathless. For me, such events reveal the wisdom of continuing to express appreciation and affection for those we love, even when we think all is lost.

Thanksgiving

Laurie Statler and her grandmother, Grace Sherman, had always been very close. At age 98, Grace's mind was devastated by Alzheimer's dementia. She didn't recognize her granddaughter or anyone else in her life.

On Thanksgiving 1998, a year before Grace would die, Laurie and her husband, Alex, with their young sons in tow, had driven from Indianapolis to Urbana to spend the holiday with Laurie's family, including Grandma Grace.

"When I was a young girl I was closer to my grandmother than to anyone else," Laurie explained. "She lived about four blocks away and I would go over to her house every day after school and stay until my parents got home from work. She sang 'Birdy with a Yellow Bill' to me and read to me from her favorite books. I still have her copy of Robert Louis Stevenson's *A Child's Garden of Verses*. She also taught me to play gin rummy. She was a wiz. I was never able to beat her. She taught me the few things I know about cooking and baking. I didn't just love her; I loved spending time with her."

When her grandmother was widowed, Laurie's father prevailed upon his mother to live with them. She wanted her independence, however. Within a year, she had moved out of her son's house and set up a new life on her own.

Through her eighties, Grace drove, gardened, and even started a new job as a docent for the local art museum. Within six months, she began a romance with a member of the museum's board, an octogenarian himself, who owned a popular restaurant in Urbana. Laurie's father was scandalized (Grace made no secret of the fact that she and her boyfriend often slept together), but Laurie was tickled. The restaurateur asked for Grace's hand in marriage, but she refused. "I value my independence too much," she told Laurie. "I like things the way they are."

Grace remained active and independent into her ninth decade. However, age inevitably began to take its toll. When she was 91, arthritis and failing eyesight convinced her to move from her apartment to an assisted living facility about 15 miles from the house in which Laurie had grown up and where her own mother still lived.

After Laurie left for college and settled in Indianapolis, she saw Grace only a few times a year, but when she did, Laurie made a point of taking her out. They would go to a park or restaurant, or just drive. During a visit in 1995, Laurie noticed that her grandmother's sharp mind had lost its edge. Within three months, Grace had to move again, from the assisted living facility to a nearby nursing home. Over the next year she became increasingly demented.

Laurie recalled, "Each time I would see her it would be a little bit worse. At first she would mis-remember who people were or where she was, but aside from being muddled, she was mostly relaxed and happy. Then she went through a period of six or eight months when she was agitated and paranoid. Thankfully, that passed and she settled down to being 'pleasantly confused.'

"Thanksgiving was coming and I hadn't seen Grandma Grace in at least eight months. My mom didn't want to cook and her home was too small for our family and my sister's family. So I had the idea of taking everyone out for

Thanksgiving dinner. We found a wonderful old hotel dining room that served a full, traditional dinner and had a piano player. It should have been wonderful.

"But Grandma Grace really had no idea where she was. She kept talking to her three sisters, all of whom were long dead. She seemed happy, at least for the first couple of hours, but it was hard on the rest of us. She kept calling me 'Ma'am,' which was really hard.

"By dessert, she was cranky, insisting that she wanted to go to her sister Evelyn's house. Alex and I hurried through dinner and told her that we were going to go to Evelyn's. The kids stayed with my mom and we bundled Grandma Grace into the car and headed to the nursing home.

"On the way she was fidgety and agitated. It had been a hard day because she had been so difficult to deal with. I was disappointed until I realized that the day had really been for me, not her. I had arranged the outing because I needed the day with her. She was fine, actually, in her own world. I had upset her routine because I needed to see her. It was my way of saying thank you to her for the countless times she had been there for me.

"By the time we got to the nursing home and were wheeling her back to her room, I was feeling that I'd made a selfish mistake. We were going to get her settled in and say good-bye, and I felt awful. Alex had left for a moment to get something from the car. I helped Grandma Grace use the bathroom and was helping her off with her cardigan. She and I were standing, facing one another. All of a sudden she looked me right in the eyes and said, 'Thank you, Princess. I'm sorry this is so hard.'

"I was dumbfounded," Laurie told me. "I said, 'I love you so much, Grandma.' And she said, 'I know, I love you, too, Laurie. You have brought me so much *naches*,' she said, using the Yiddish word for joy.

"And that was it. She hugged me and I just cried in her arms. Then she was just quiet and a moment later, I was 'Ma'am' again. I'm not sure I would believe this myself. But when I turned around, Alex was at the door. He had arrived just in time to hear Grandma Grace thank me and tell me she loved me." She chuckled, "He looked stunned, like he'd witnessed a 'close encounter.'"

Her grandmother had actually known who Laurie was, at least for about 45 seconds. I've heard dozens of stories like this. Alzheimer's specialists know of similar stories. There is no neurological explanation for this phenomenon. It's as if the synapses, hopelessly tangled by dementia, suddenly unravel. People describe their demented relative stepping out of their dementia, as if it were a parallel reality or alter ego.

A common feature to these stories is that they are always profoundly meaningful to the person who relates the event. Perhaps, on some level, the person who has fallen victim to dementia feels what we need and struggles to recruit the remaining shreds of cognitive capacity to connect one last time with us.

I asked Laurie what was most important for her about her brief interaction. She hesitated and then said, "I think it was that Grandma acknowledged in her 'Thank you' that she knew how much I loved her. Until that moment, I knew she loved me—and I certainly loved her—but I wasn't sure she knew just how important she was to me."

I asked Laurie how her grandmother seemed after that day. "Oh, much the same. I saw her every couple of months until she died. But there was never another moment like that. Still, it was okay. We had said what we needed to; nothing was lacking. There was this wonderful sense of closure. When I think of Grandma Grace, I remember her just as she was at that moment."

The value of saying thank you transcends knowing whether or not the sentiment has been received. Even if thanks had not been returned, it would have been worthwhile for Laurie to say thank you to her grandmother.

Every culture and faith tradition recognizes the critical value of expressing gratitude with prayers of thanksgiving and blessings for the gift of life. The absence of gratitude can erode a person's health and quality of life. Elie Wiesel, a concentration camp survivor who went on to win the Nobel Peace Prize, has suggested that, "When a person doesn't have gratitude, something is missing in his or her humanity."

Parents of infants who have died have told me how important it was for them to say thank you to their baby for having been a gift of joy in their lives. They know that their child can't understand their words, but they have told me that they nonetheless sense that their dead child felt their gratitude and love.

CHAPTER THIRTEEN

The Family Dynamics of Gratitude

I have long thought that the phrase *dysfunctional family* is redundant. Family life tends to be messy. Boundaries of privacy that are expected in other relationships simply don't exist within families. Parents and children commonly intrude in one another's personal affairs. This is appropriate when children are young. Parents set the agenda, and young children interrupt their parents with problems at any time. But difficulties in the relationships will inevitably arise if kids remain dependent into adulthood or parents continue to be intrusive or controlling.

Family dynamics are just that, dynamic. As individuals grow and develop over time, so, too, relationships naturally change. They must if they are to remain healthy—or become healthy. Therein lies hope for us all.

The wisdom within the Four Things can help a child and parent remove any and all barriers to the love they share. Gratitude can be both a vehicle and an earned reward for accepting and nurturing one another.

Arlene, a colleague of mine, learned this lesson when she helped care for her stepfather at the end of his life, a man to whom she had never felt particularly close.

We were working together on a study of how a son or daughter experiences caring for a terminally ill parent. "This project is hitting close to home," Arlene said and sighed. "But in my case, it wasn't my father who was dying, but my stepfather. And when I heard that he was finally dying, my first response was 'Good! It's long overdue!' I never thought his death would end up transforming me or completely recasting my relationship to him, my mother, and, for that matter, his children as well."

Failure of the Heart

Arlene's parents divorced when she was eight. An alcoholic, her father moved away after the divorce and Arlene hardly saw him. Her mother, Hazel, was single for eight years and so reclusive and shy that Arlene assumed she would never remarry.

Hazel's temperament perfectly suited her vocation as porcelain sculptor, but severely constricted her social circle. She met Conrad, a surgeon who painted watercolors as a hobby, at a juried art show at which they both had work on display. She was in her midforties, he a few years older. His eye was captured first by Hazel's work and then her delicate features.

Because Conrad was married when he met Hazel, they didn't get involved. Conrad's wife was usually isolated from him and their children because of severe depression. She was often suicidal and occasionally had to be hospitalized. For months at a time she lived in supervised housing for her own safety. Conrad eventually divorced, later saw Hazel at a local art opening, and asked her out.

Arlene recalled that, even after her mother and Conrad were married, she never fully trusted him or his motives. "It always irritated me as a child when we'd have company and he'd say that he had been 'smitten' with my mother at that first meeting because he was married at the time. He meant to be endearing, but it grated at me. It felt wrong. My mother kept quiet, which always made it seem as though the feeling was mutual, but I assumed she was quiet because she was so introverted. I couldn't imagine that she would have the slightest interest in a married man. I guess I felt Conrad had somehow manipulated my mother and I turned it into a grudge."

The year of their courtship was during Arlene's first year of junior high school. She remembered sitting in the kitchen doing homework. Her mother came flitting into the room. Arlene said she had never seen her mother flit! Hazel was humming and pulled out her sewing kit. It seemed she had offered to mend a couple of things for Conrad. Arlene couldn't believe it. This was a side of her mother she had not seen and could never have imagined.

"Soon it was clear that my mother had fallen head over heels in love with him," she said. "Not me. I never fully trusted him. Maybe it was because my mother seemed beside herself—on cloud nine. She had always been so contained. So considered. Now she seemed giddy, and, to my adolescent eyes, more than a little bit silly. He tried to connect with me, I suppose, but they were so caught up in each other. I felt excluded, as though I were an encumbrance. It was difficult for me, after having my mother to myself all those years."

"How did he try to connect with you?" I asked.

"He would sometimes take me with him to the hospital. He encouraged my interest in science. It's really because of him that I pursued biology and research."

"So he did have positive influence on you."

"Yes. But I couldn't accept it or allow myself to really see it at the time."

At 63, Conrad suddenly became sick, just as Arlene was entering graduate school. "He almost died those first few days," Arlene recalled. "But during the next ten years he was like Lazarus, dying and arising again and again."

Conrad had been stricken with viral myocarditis, an infection of the heart muscle caused by a variant of a common cold germ. Overnight his heart lost its power to pump, his blood pressure dropped dangerously low, and fluid backed up in his lungs. He spent two weeks in the ICU of the hospital in which he practiced. The doctors and nurses hovered, making sure that no stone was unturned in the quest for a cure. Over time he gradually improved, except for occasional cardiac arrhythmias, episodes of fluttering in his heart, during which his blood pressure bottomed out. Without a quick push of the right IV drugs or an electrical jolt to his chest, any one of these episodes could kill him.

Before leaving the hospital, he needed a pacemaker, a combination of pills, and, after nearly dying on two occasions, an internal defibrillator.

Conrad was grateful for every day. His father had died at 57 and no man in his family had lived beyond the age of 60. On every one of his next 10 birthdays he would make a toast and say, "This life is a gift to me. Thank you for being part of it."

"In retrospect I realize his gratitude was sincere," said Arlene. "But, at the time, my mistrust of him made it seem contrived and somehow phony."

Soon after Conrad's seventy-third birthday, he began to have headaches. An MRI showed multiple small brain tumors, characteristic of cancer that has started elsewhere. A search for the source tumor (which is often found in the colon or lung) didn't turn up anything. There was nothing to do but control symptoms and make good use of the time left. Conrad had radiation treatments to his brain and for a few months did fairly well, though the edges of his intellect dulled and he gradually became dependent on Arlene for basic things, such as dressing and using the toilet.

"My mother was a mess," said Arlene. "I was living nearby so I was often around. My stepfather gradually lost interest in eating. His cardiologist, who was also a good friend of theirs, suggested getting hospice involved. Mom wouldn't hear of it. To her it would have meant giving up."

This is an all-too-common situation. Medicare and many insurance plans typically will only pay for hospice care after a seriously ill person agrees to forgo life-prolonging treatment. As a result, in the United States hospice has become associated with "giving up." It's too bad because hospice provides a long list of services that sick people and their families need, including in-home nursing and bathing, and 24/7 emergency support for family caregivers.

"One day Mom found Conrad on the floor, delirious," Arlene continued. "She called me from the hospital that night. 'I can't do this anymore,' I remember her saying."

It turned out that the emergency department physician on duty that evening had told Hazel soon after Conrad was admitted that her husband was probably dying. He remained incoherent and looked as if he might die at any moment. Conrad's cardiologist and friend admitted him to the hospital and sat with Hazel for several hours. He suggested to her that it might be time to consider turning off Conrad's internal defibrillator. Conrad was unconscious at the time.

Hazel contacted Arlene and then Conrad's children late that night and conveyed the details of his condition and the doctor's suggestions as carefully as she could.

His children didn't ask many questions, but by the next afternoon they were at the hospital in force and in foul moods.

"I hardly knew Conrad's children from his first marriage," Arlene explained. "I'd met Florence, the youngest, but his sons, Edward and Stafford, were in their late twenties during the time of the divorce and his courtship with Mom. There was no tradition of holidays or anything else that brought us together, so I hardly ever saw them. I always assumed that it was their choice. They always seemed miffed so I wasn't about to reach out. I suspected that they blamed Mom for causing the divorce, which was ridiculous, of course.

"Stafford and Florence were at the hospital when the oncologist made rounds and cheerfully remarked that he thought Dad would do well with a new treatment. His children had been suspicious that Mom wasn't feeding him enough; now they were horror-struck to think she'd considered turning off the defibrillator."

After two days of intravenous fluids and a new medication, Conrad was indeed more alert and mostly coherent, and his children's suspicions deepened. Meanwhile, the hospital abruptly sent him home.

"Mom felt she was being unfairly attacked by Conrad's children and withdrew even further into herself. At the hospital, his children would avoid us and talk only with him. But then Conrad's brother, Roger, came over to the house.

"He sat me down in the kitchen. 'You know,' he said, 'Conrad's children would really like to come visit. But they don't feel welcome in your mother's home. They want to be part of this, but they're afraid of your mother.' I almost laughed. My mother is all of five foot one. Although she looks strong willed, she is totally timid. Roger said, 'Do you know that they have never once been invited to dinner at your mother's home? Not once in over twenty-five years of marriage?'

"And it hit me—that was true! I had never thought about it. But Mom's social phobias, her insecurities about cooking, and her assumptions about what his children thought of her made her shrink from any such prospect. And Conrad deferred to her, his porcelain wife."

Arlene didn't defend her mother, but did explain that what Conrad's children understandably felt to be disdain was nothing of the sort. Her mother was intimidated by the thought of them. In a sense, Conrad was at fault. He could have asserted himself and simply insisted on having his children visit. Arlene was sure that her mother would have been fine once her shyness gave way to familiarity. By being overly protective, Conrad had made matters worse.

Arlene immediately became resolute. She asked Roger to tell Conrad's children that they were welcome at any time in her mother's house and invited them to come over that evening. When they arrived, she told them they were welcome at any time. Hazel didn't resist at all. She seemed relieved that Arlene had taken matters into her own hands. Arlene's emotional transformation was just beginning.

"At first I felt ashamed for my part in keeping them away. As I opened our home to them, someplace within me opened as well," said Arlene. "The distrust and low-grade animosity I'd always felt for my stepfather eased. For the first time I was able to stand outside 'my own story' and look at the history of our family from his perspective. And for the first time I understood how much he really and truly loved my mom. To protect her from his own kids! Then I realized how much I had lost in holding myself aloof and apart from him and my stepsiblings.

"At one point, I looked over at Florence, who was sitting with her eyes swollen and both hands wrapped tightly around a hot cup of tea. I said, 'I'm so sorry I didn't know you and your brothers before now. I feel like it's my fault.' I watched as tears poured down her cheeks. I started bawling, too, got up, and hugged her."

Rewriting History

The scene Arlene described was a true watershed moment. From that point on, the adult children were on the same side and decided to take charge of Conrad's care and support Hazel together.

Learning to relate to adult stepsiblings whom we didn't know as children is a challenge that has become fairly common in contemporary families. Yet it's one of those things for which my generation, the boomers, haven't had many role models. I'm not faulting our parents; we simply live in different times. It's one example of many situations in which we boomers are faced with figuring out things for ourselves in order to live fully, honestly, and responsibly. The way Arlene and her stepsiblings handled this predicament offers essential wisdom for all of us.

I asked Arlene if her stepsiblings had been able to say any of the Four Things to Conrad before he died.

"To an extent they did. But they really had a hard time asking for what they needed. They didn't know how. Conrad was old school in a lot of ways. He wasn't able to be direct in saying 'I love you' or those sorts of things to his children. I don't think he ever realized that they were waiting for some words of approval or forgiveness from him. But they were able to forgive my mom and even express real warmth and affection for her. In a way, I think that helped them feel complete with their father."

Arlene explained that Conrad's kids realized during those days just how much in love Conrad and Hazel had always been. They recalled how their father and Hazel held hands as they walked and cuddled whenever they sat together. Conrad's children no longer saw Hazel as a malevolent force but instead a meek soon-to-be widow. Conrad's oldest son told Arlene that if responsibility needed to be assigned for the decades-long chasm that cut through their family's history, his father was mostly to blame.

Anger and blame gave way to the fact that their father was dying.

"Day by day more of him leaked away," said Arlene. "In his weakness, his edges softened and each day his disposition seemed more innocent and childlike. He was a pleasure to take care of, even though taking care of him was a lot of work."

Once they were home from the hospital for the last time, Hazel was able to accept hospice's help. The hospice team arranged for an electric hospital bed and a bedside commode and gave them instructions on how to use medication to alleviate discomfort and confusion.

Arlene explained that in the last few days of his life, Conrad was sometimes in a world of his own. He would seem very busy, muttering to himself and making hand gestures as though he were conducting an "air orchestra." Although he was usually calm, he occasionally became agitated, trying to get out of bed and saying, "I need to go home now. Help me get ready!"

"At one point," said Arlene, "Conrad was trying to get out of bed and Mom was leaning over and talking to him quietly. He grabbed her shoulders with both hands. She was frightened. 'Conrad, it's me—Hazel. Sweetheart, you're here with me. You're fine, darling. It's all right.' He looked up in recognition, relaxed his hold, and smiled at her. He reached up, put his arms around her neck, pulled her down, and gave her a long kiss.

"'I love you, Hazel,' he said. 'I love you, too, darling,' my mom replied.

"'I've been so happy,' he said. 'How can I thank you for these years together? It has been wonderful to be married to you.' He paused for a second and exclaimed, 'I want to do it again!'

"She looked at him and I could tell she was too moved to speak. 'Will you be my lawfully wedded wife?' he asked. She nodded. 'Always,' she managed to say. He smiled broadly and then floated again off into another world."

"Did your mother say anything to you at the time?" I asked.

"Not at first. We just looked at one another. Mom's eyes welled with tears. Then I said, 'He is the great love of your life, isn't he?' And she said, 'Yes, he is my great love.'

"Suddenly, when she said that, it was as if whatever lingering resentment or distrust I felt for him fell away. I felt this overwhelming feeling of gratitude. He had made my mother incredibly happy. He meant so much to her. I recognized in a flash that she had her own life apart from me. At that moment I grew up the rest of the way in my relationship with my mom—and with my stepfather.

"The next time Conrad was lucid, I went and sat with him. My mom was reading in his room and I asked her if I could have some time alone with him. She was surprised but seemed pleased and left us. I then apologized to him for being so difficult for so long, and I thanked him for loving my mother. 'You have made her so happy,' I said to him. 'Thank you.'

"He just smiled at me and reached out his hand, which required a significant effort for him at the time. He nodded and said, 'I know. I know.' And I realized that he had always been aware of my animosity and mistrust toward him, but accepted it as something he couldn't change. He had honored my right to have my own feelings, even if they were unfair toward him. What a generous thing that was! I thanked him again and, for the first time in our lives together, I kissed his cheek.

"That evening he died. He had been restless and breathing irregularly and he suddenly started to sit up. He stared ahead as if trying to discern something in the distance and took one last breath. Just then my mother came into the room. I turned off the oxygen machine and the room was suddenly quiet and still. Mom kissed his forehead and then climbed into bed and held him. She lay there with her hand on his cheek, her body molded to his."

Losing a Stepfather, Gaining a Family

The church at Conrad's funeral was overflowing with family, friends, colleagues, and patients. The day after the funeral, Conrad's children returned to Hazel's house for a few hours. There were things to organize and notes to write acknowledging and thanking people who had helped during the long months.

"When it came time to leave, it was very hard. We were all hugging one another—mom, too! Conrad's children had all made the transition from being strangers to being relatives. We realized that we are connected. The feeling of gratitude I had toward Conrad when he kissed my mother had spilled over and I felt open, utterly forgiving, thankful, and even loving toward them. It was amazing."

Gratitude was the vehicle for Arlene's journey from being the victim of a fractured family to feeling part of a family that was healthy and whole. In allowing herself to feel gratitude to Conrad for his unwavering love and devotion to her mother, the walls of anger that separated Arlene from Conrad and her stepsiblings dissolved. With her defenses down, Arlene suddenly felt thankful for all the things he had done for her mother, and she was surprised at the love she felt for him. In the course of Conrad's dying, Arlene gained the stepfather she never realized she had, and in the process she also discovered two brothers and a sister she will have for the rest of her life.

Arlene observed, "I wish I hadn't waited so long, but it took Conrad's dying for me to discover that I really have a family."

Anger constrains our options. If pain and regrets make you see only the wounds and ways of defending yourself from being hurt again, practicing gratitude—starting with gratitude for life itself—can expand your perspective on the world and your options for living. In no longer acting from woundedness, you will regain emotional balance and control of your interactions. Without minimizing the pain of the past, your own healing will become possible.

Arlene said, "My stepfather's death was one of the most important events in my life, up there with my marriage and the birth of my children. It was truly healing. Ironically, in his dying, things happened within our family that he most wished for in his life."

Marie de Hennezel, a psychologist who works with cancer and AIDS patients in Paris, has observed, "Life has taught me three things: The first is that I cannot escape my own death or the deaths of the people I love. The second is that no human being can be reduced to what we see, or think we see. Any person is infinitely larger, and deeper, than our narrow judgments can discern. And third: He or she can never be considered to have uttered the final word on anything, is always developing, always has the power of self-fulfillment, and a capacity for self-transformation through all the crises and trials of life."

Our human potential can be nurtured at any time in life. I asked Arlene how her experience influenced her current life. She said, "The life lessons for me were about responsibility and creativity. We didn't have family traditions or religious customs for dealing with my stepfather's dying or his funeral. I took responsibility because someone had to, but at first I felt lost without a rudder. Then I realized it was alright to make it up as we went along, to be creative about taking responsibility. We wrote this chapter in his life

and our family's life the way we wanted the story to un-
fold."

Arlene's attitude of creative responsibility for her relationships and life continues to be an important theme for her
and her family. "In addition to consciously creating family
relationships with Conrad's children, my family has begun
designing our own rituals. We draw on timeless traditions,
but work together to create something new, that has meaning for us. For instance, we held a rite of passage for my
son, Chad, when he turned thirteen. We discussed and designed the event together. We gathered with relatives and
friends at a park that has been part of Chad's life since he
was an infant. People read passages or poems they had chosen for the occasion and offered Chad some piece of wisdom. It was a wonderfully warm and heartfelt occasion, as
well as a funny and joyous celebration of Chad at this time
of transformation in his life. In his gracious acceptance,
laughter, and poise, I saw my son mature that day."

We should never underestimate the possibility for change
and growth in any human being. Emotional health and
happiness are ours to create. When we reach, as Arlene did,
to nurture and complete our most important relationships,
we are practicing self-care, as well as extending an ines-
timable gift to others.

PART FOUR

I Love You

What keeps us alive, what allows us to endure?
I think it is the hope of loving,
Or being loved.

MEISTER ECKHART,
Love Poems from God
(TRANSLATED BY DANIEL LADINSKY)

Introduction

Love is the most powerful of human emotions. And "I love you" is arguably the single most important sentence in any language.

"Love is its own because!" declared a student in a high school class that I taught one day. I had asked the students why they thought love between people is so important. The response, while perhaps not grammatically correct, is true. In rejecting the question, the student gave the correct answer. Love requires no justification. It has inherent value. If you love someone, no other reason for loving—or living— is needed.

When death approaches, saying "I love you" is a supremely life-affirming, almost defiant, act. It is a way of declaring that our relationships matter. Dying patients have shown me this again and again in the ways that they choose to spend their limited energy and fleeting time. They intuitively grasp that our connections to each other are what matter most.

As important as it is—maybe because it is so important—"I love you" can also be the three most difficult words for us to say. But sometimes when certain words are hard to come by, people find other ways to express the love that is in their hearts.

CHAPTER FOURTEEN

Creative Ways of Saying the Four Things

Gunter, a colleague of mine at the University of Montana, and Edie, his wife, came to see me at my office with questions about the care of Gunter's elderly father. They were headed to Gunter's hometown in Minnesota for what they expected would be the last time they would see his dad, who had been diagnosed with multiple myeloma, a cancer of the bone marrow and blood, and was declining rapidly. Gunter's stepmother could no longer care for him, and, although she hated to, had placed him in a nursing home.

We spoke about serious matters having to do with CPR and do-not-resuscitate orders, antibiotics for infections, artificial nutrition by tube, palliative care, and hospice. When, in the course of the consultation, I introduced the Four

Things, Gunter said, "Yes, *but what if you're Lutheran*?" His pleading tone and pained expression were meant to be comical, but he was not entirely kidding.

A Creative Approach to Expressing Love

Gunter's father came from a long line of stoic German farmers. He grew up in a loving family, but there was no tradition of openly expressing affection.

"There were unspoken, but clear, rules. We never said, 'I love you' to one another. I might write 'I love you' on my mother's birthday card, but that's about it. In my family, hugs are perfunctory. We lean forward so that we barely touch."

Edie piped in, "Actually, Gunter's been in recovery since marrying me. He's had to get in touch with his 'inner Italian.'" She leaned over and gave him a sloppy kiss on the cheek. "My maiden name is Catalano," she explained.

"Her family is the polar opposite of mine," said Gunter. "Within a half hour of meeting Edie's extended family, one of her aunts was pinching my cheeks! I'd only seen that in the movies!"

Edie laughed, "He's even learned to talk with his hands."

Often when I talk with patients or their family members about the value of expressing love and affection in completing relationships, they say, "Yes, but in our family that's just not done." Cultures communicate differently; some are clearly more emotionally expressive than others. German Lutherans are not known for exuberant displays of affection. There are gender differences, too. Men may be more reticent than women when it comes to saying "I love you." That doesn't mean they don't feel love or have other healthy ways of expressing it.

I suggested to Gunter and Edie that there are lots of ways to communicate the Four Things. "I've known people who tape-recorded a message," I said, "because it was too hard to do in person. It's not always necessary to say the Four Things in person. Sometimes people find it easier to write them in a letter. The point is to communicate forgiveness, gratitude, and love in a way the person you're communicating with can understand. The more explicit you are, the better."

Since there was no precedent for this sort of communication in Gunter's family, Gunter and Edie realized that they would need to be creative in their approach to his father. They promised to let me know how things went.

Four days later Gunter called me in the evening from Minnesota.

"Hi, Ira. Sorry to bother you at home, but Edie convinced me you'd want to hear this!" He was obviously excited. "This afternoon the most incredible thing happened."

His father was indeed dying. The nursing home physician with whom they spoke didn't think he would live out the month. He was comfortable but very weak when they first arrived. Gunter and Edie took a motel room (they didn't want to inconvenience Gunter's stepmother) and settled in for the duration.

"We went back to see him the following morning. He wanted to discuss practical matters. There was his medical directive to complete and some property and business issues that he and my stepmother had asked us to handle. Imagine my surprise when he asked Edie to have some time with me alone. I had no idea what was coming. 'Son, would you please shave me?' he asked.

"I didn't know what to say. It was completely unexpected. For weeks he'd been shaved each morning by my stepmom or an aide. Thanks to our conversation, Ira, I recognized this was an opportunity.

"I know my father well. His illness hadn't dulled his mental faculties and he would *never* do anything without planning every detail. There was no doubt whatsoever in my mind that he knew exactly what he was doing. He had deliberately waited for me that morning. I realized that my father was really asking me to touch him."

Gunter gathered towels, shaving cream, and a basin and set about the task. An aide helped him transfer his father into a special reclining chair used for shampooing residents' hair.

Gunter said that seeing his father reclining in the chair, eyes closed, completely helpless, brought him to the verge of tears, but he postponed them because he had a job to do. He took his time, starting with a hot towel, like the barbers used to use. He told his dad it was "to soften up his beard," but he really did it because he knew it would feel good. He decided to make the shaving into a ritual—a way to say I love you to his father—and good-bye.

He draped the towel over his father's face and let it sit.

The two men barely spoke, but they were communicating. "My father's beard felt like sandpaper under my fingertips," said Gunter. "As I massaged his face, I felt the firm ripples of his jaw muscles soften and noted that his shoulders relaxed under the towels that I had draped around him."

Gunter said it felt a bit strange at first to touch his father's face in such an intimate, tender way. He took his father's old shaving brush, cup, and special shaving soap, and worked up a rich, smooth lather. It had been many years since he'd used a cup and brush rather than shaving foam that came out of an aerosol can, but it came back to him. The smell of the shaving soap—the same brand that his father had used all his life—transported Gunter back to his childhood. As he stood behind his father and shaved the front of his neck, chills ran up his spine. He realized that they were replaying a scene from his childhood.

"My father's birthday present to me when I was thirteen was a Gillette safety razor," said Gunter. "That morning he showed me how to shave for the first time. He stood behind me in front of the bathroom mirror and showed me how to scoop the lather up as I shaved my neck. It was an important rite of passage for me at the time. I realized that we were conducting a rite of passage for my father."

I asked how his father had responded.

"Mostly he just rested with his eyes closed. For a moment I thought he might fall asleep. I finished by washing his face and massaged him again as I applied aftershave cream.

"As I sat him up in the chair, he said, 'Thank you, Gunter, that feels much better.' I made a point of looking into his eyes and said, 'You're welcome, Dad. If you'd like, tomorrow morning I'll bring scissors and trim the hairs around your ears.' 'I'd like that,' he replied."

"What an experience!" I remarked.

"Ira, it's hard to express what a breakthrough this is. We both knew that this wasn't about being shaved, it was about being touched. Because of our discussion in your office, it was possible for me to hear what he was really requesting. It was something that he needed, and it was obviously something *I* needed. Touching him was magical. We communicated more love to each other today than we have in all our lives."

When I next spoke to Gunter, he had just returned from Minnesota. His father had died about two and a half weeks after they had arrived. Gunter said that he had shaved his father every day, and, as his dad became weaker, he took on more of the tasks of his physical care. Combing his father's hair was a natural extension of Gunter's foray into barbering. Since he spent most of each day at the nursing home, it was also only natural for him to begin helping his father dress each morning. The first week of their visit, Gunter encouraged his father to have a bit of soup or pudding, and he helped him to the toilet. By the end of the second week, he was feeding his father and helping him with a bedpan and then with adult diapers. Gunter reflected that his father had once done the same for him, changing his diapers and patiently spoon-feeding him. They had come full circle. Gunter described his final visit with his father as, "quite simply, the best time we've ever had together."

I asked Gunter how his father's gift of touch had affected him.

"Every time I think about it I feel a rush of gratitude and love," Gunter said. "The sadness at his death is there, but so is this intense joy at the ways in which we were able to connect in those final days."

Physical Love

Physical affection is often equated with sex. But there are many forms of physical love. Think of a mother bathing and playing with her giggling baby. So, too, at the end of life, we have an opportunity to pamper those we love with physical comfort, even physical pleasure.

There was nothing romantic—in any sense of the word—about the care that Gunter gave to his father. But there is no denying that it was a physical expression of love. So, too, was his father's request to Gunter, and his receptivity to Gunter's loving touch.

We can learn a lot about caring for frail, elderly people from the way we care for infants who are entirely dependent on us. Naturally, we feed them and make sure they are clean and dry, but we also actively love them. It happens even in clinical settings. A crying infant in the emergency department is not merely examined for physical problems: the baby is held and rocked. We reflexively hold and touch infants not merely to relieve their suffering, but to elicit pleasure. There is no reason why we cannot do the same for people who are physically dependent on us at the end of life.

In fact, the phrase *tender, loving care* is the sine qua non of excellence in caring. It's true for every culture. Excellent medical care for dying people is essential, but it is not sufficient. Loving care is a hallmark of human caring.

By "loving" I do mean not merely a comfortable environment, like the lighting or temperature in a room. *Love* is an active verb. Authentic loving care involves touching people tenderly. Touching people who are ill or debilitated for the sake of their comfort and even to elicit pleasure is entirely wholesome. We don't do nearly enough of it.

Gunter's experience reveals another aspect of loving care—that it is deeply meaningful and satisfying for those who do the caring. This holds true for relatives, friends, and for doctors, nurses, and nurse's aides. This drive to love is, in fact, what calls the best professionals to their vocations. To love someone, and have him or her accept your love, is profoundly meaningful, and, at no time is this more important than at the end of life.

There is no "right way" to say thank you, I love you, and good-bye. Each of us has a style of communication that feels natural for us. These communication styles are influenced by our culture, upbringing, and gender. The story of Gunter shaving his father reminds us that not all communication needs to be verbal. Sometimes touch and actions speak as loudly, and more clearly, than words ever could.

CHAPTER FIFTEEN

Loving the Body

Sometimes in the most difficult situations imaginable, love does conquer all.

In his letter to the Corinthians, the apostle Paul speaks of the most important things in life: "Faith, hope and love. . . . But the greatest of these is love." Twenty centuries later, John Lennon's lyric "All you need is love" became a generation's anthem. Nowadays that seems simplistic. Love seems impotent in the face of natural disasters and disease, and an anemic response to the human problems of war and poverty. Still, when relationships are strained, and in situations in which faith is sorely tested and hope seems lost, Paul's ancient wisdom rings true.

A Commitment to Love

Several years ago, I learned of an older couple who had cared for a son dying of AIDS. I was involved with the case indirectly, through supervision and suggestions to the hospice team and doctor, but the more I learned about it, the more interested I became. Much more than another tragic account of AIDS, the circumstances surrounding Mike Whitman's dying were so extraordinary that a year after he died, I contacted his parents directly to ask if they would talk with me about their son's passing. I wanted to hear about it firsthand and meet the people whose commitment to love had become almost archetypal in my mind.

Horace and Louise Whitman are Christian fundamentalists who raised four children and devoted their lives to their church. Mike and his three sisters attended Christian elementary schools and a Christian university in Oklahoma. Following college, Mike lived in Oregon and California, and then, around age 35, returned to Missoula. On the surface he led the life of a God-fearing, dutiful son. He worked as a paralegal, sang in the church choir, and taught Bible studies on the weekend. His apartment along the Clark Fork River was within walking distance of his parents' house, and he had dinner with them several nights a week.

When Mike didn't show up for work one day, his sister found him in his apartment weak and disoriented. He was immediately hospitalized, given a battery of tests, and was found to have AIDS, already in an advanced stage.

Horace and Louise were, needless to say, stunned to

learn about Mike's illness. Their first response was long periods of prayer. They had no inkling that their son was gay;
even the idea of homosexuality was repugnant to them.

At the time AIDS treatment was still fairly primitive;
the newer so-called HAART drugs—for Highly Active
Anti-Retroviral Treatment—were years away. Mike's condition was clearly terminal. He was in the hospital for a
week or so, and, during this time, he and his parents had
momentous decisions to make: Who would care for him
and where?

Horace and Louise were ashamed of their son's disease
and what it symbolized to them. Their honesty demanded
that they acknowledge the deep wound in their relationship
with him, a relationship they had thought was whole. They
were caught in a soul-wrenching tension between the
tenets of their faith and their love for their son. They could
not make him right in their eyes or the eyes of their church,
but they could not deny their love.

Many people profess to "hate the sin, love the sinner,"
but few are tested as were the Whitmans. Confronted with
the choice of rejecting or embracing their son, the Whitmans' response was instantaneous and unequivocal: they
wanted to take care of Mike in their home. "There was no
other way to go," Louise said. "We loved Mike, we loved
him dearly, and we still do. We wanted to do everything we
could for him ourselves."

While their feelings about homosexuality were no secret, no one at the hospital ever heard a word of rebuke
from the Whitmans or detected a shred of doubt in their
decision.

When I asked the Whitmans about their interactions with Mike in the hospital, Horace cocked his head to one side and shrugged, relating his discussion in a matter-of-fact manner: "I told him that I could not condone what he had done. I'll never understand it. But I said, 'I love you, son. That will never change.' Really, that was it."

"What did Mike say?" I asked.

"Well," said Horace, "he just looked sad. He said 'I love you, too' and that he was sorry to be causing us pain." Horace's voice broke.

For his part, Mike chose to come home out of love. He could have gone to the home of a gay couple, friends who had offered to care for him. They lived out of town and he would not have had to face his parents' shame. Even though they seldom spoke of it, or showed it, he knew his homosexuality had ripped apart his parents' image of him and their family, and caused them to feel dishonored in their faith community. By letting his mother and father care for him, he could, in some measure, restore their parental role.

Nonetheless, there was nothing neat or pretty about the situation with Mike and his family. Mike's parents wanted him to recant his homosexuality and make a public apology to their congregation. Mike's gay friends wanted to care for him—and they wanted to see him—and they were deeply hurt at being excluded from his parents' home.

In the midst of all this, the Whitman's love for their son shone like a beacon. Mike had a slew of physical problems, including rectal herpes lesions that required frequent cleaning. The image is indelibly etched in my mind of Horace Whitman gently bathing his son's sores three times a day, knowing full well what had caused them, and believing, as he did, that homosexuality was a sin. He did this without a whisper of scolding. Mike was his son and it was a job that needed to be done.

At its root a parent's love for his or her child knows no bounds. It is an impulse that is both primal and transcendent. The same is true of a child's love for his parents. This kind of love is not volitional. It is who we are. We belong to one another and that, it seems to me, is the best part of being alive.

People are often put off by trappings of illness: the tubes, pill bottles, bedside commodes, bedpans, and the unpleasant odors and visible physical decline. In modern times, the tendency has been to avoid all that by turning care over to hospitals and the people in white who work within them. By trying to sanitize illness and dying we inadvertently separate and isolate the people we love—and we isolate ourselves. Isolation is the opposite of loving connection.

Caring for people who are dying is never as bad as it seems at first. I had a certain squeamishness when I had to change my daughter's first diapers, but I soon got over it. The hands-on care needed at the end of life often involves similar tasks that take some getting used to. But it's not that big of a deal.

We may avoid people who are dying because on a subconscious level of magical thinking we worry that death is somehow contagious. We shouldn't worry—we're already infected! We are all HMG positive (the human mortality gene). No one is getting out of this one alive. In our culture

of mouthwashes, deodorants, sanitary napkins, disinfec-
tants, and dry cleaners, it's easy to forget that we're animals.
Being an animal has many advantages (it's vastly preferable
to being a mineral or vegetable), but it means that as people
approach the end of their lives, they may well need help
with their basic bodily functions. When we love someone,
we have to love *all* of them, including their animal nature
and eventual physical dependence. We will all, in due time,
have to love that part of ourselves, too.

In his *Letters to a Young Poet,* Rainer Maria Rilke wrote:
"For one human being to love another human being: that is
perhaps the most difficult task that has been entrusted to
us, the ultimate test and proof, the work for which all other
work is merely preparation." When we feel the burden of
love, how difficult and demanding it can be at times, we can
take inspiration from the Whitmans.

CHAPTER SIXTEEN

Living Every Day as if It Were Your First—or Last

When life is short, each moment can become precious and perfect. We shouldn't have to wait for death's approach to realize this essential truth of living. When we come fully into the present, moment to moment, we have the sense that we're living life to the fullest and each moment is a celebration. The courage of Gabrielle, a young girl who developed cancer, drove home this point to me.

Like many childhood cancers, Gabrielle's illness began with minor complaints that simply didn't get better. Flu-like symptoms, achy joints, low-grade fever, and general tiredness started in midweek and lasted through the weekend. On a Monday in 1992, Yvette took her 12-year-old daughter to their family's pediatrician in their small, largely French-speaking, northern New Hampshire community.

The doctor diagnosed a viral illness and said that despite a negative Monospot office test, Gabrielle probably had mononucleosis. But she injected a note of caution, saying that Gabrielle's white blood cell count was very high. She'd want to repeat her blood test in a few weeks to make sure things had returned to normal.

Yvette recalled feeling that something was wrong, "I was frightened, as if I intuitively knew it was more serious than just a cold."

After two weeks of fluids, bed rest, and Tylenol, Gabrielle wasn't getting better. Another trip to the pediatrician resulted in further reassurance and encouragement. But at three weeks the tests for "mono" were still negative and Gabrielle's white blood cell count was still sky-high. The need to "make sure this is not leukemia" was mentioned and more tests ordered. A bone marrow aspirate was performed, which showed that Gabrielle indeed had "acute lymphocytic leukemia."

The diagnosis left Gabrielle and her family shocked, but they had no thought of Gabrielle dying, only that they needed to do whatever was necessary to defeat the disease. Curing Gabrielle's leukemia became the central focus for Yvette; Gabrielle's father, Adam; her six-year-old brother, Claude; and her three-year-old sister, Sylvie.

Two days later they drove two and a quarter hours to the regional cancer center and met Dr. deMontigny, a specialist in childhood leukemias. Recent advances in leukemia treatment gave them every reason to be hopeful. Dr. deMontigny told them there was a good chance that Gabrielle would be cured and wanted to start her on an experimental protocol of medications in cycles, which he felt was the best treatment available. He warned that the treatment would take three years to complete and would be difficult at times.

It was.

"The regimen was arduous," recalled Yvette. "Gabrielle had to be in the hospital for weeks at a time. I stayed with her. Mostly, though, she was on a schedule of medications at home, and she could attend school."

Childhood leukemia used to be uniformly fatal, but potent medications and bone marrow transplants have been developed. Today, many children are cured of the disease.

Gabrielle's treatment consisted of high doses of "cytotoxic chemotherapy," medications designed to kill fast-dividing cancer cells in her bone marrow. Unfortunately, the medicine also killed other rapidly dividing cells of her immune system and the cells lining her mouth, esophagus, intestines, and hair follicles. During peaks in the cycles of chemotherapy, she sometimes had mouth and throat sores and diarrhea. For months at a time, she lost every hair on her body. "Getting shiny" is what she called it.

When the final course of chemotherapy was over, everyone celebrated with a pizza party for their family and Gabrielle's friends. But, within a month, the aches and fever had returned. Blood tests revealed that Gabrielle's leukemia had recurred. The family's bright hopes came crashing down.

Dr. deMontigny was also disappointed and explained that they were now on the downside of the statistical see-saw. Since the leukemia had bounced back from the strong cancer medications, a cure was unlikely. Gabrielle was composed during the meeting and asked questions about what the various treatments would entail and how they would make her feel.

None of her options were good. Cancer doctors give the best, most effective medications they have first. When those treatments fail, the second-line alternatives are not likely to work, at least not for long. Dr. deMontigny laid out the available regimens, usually combining two or three medications, and explained how each would control the leukemia, its common side effects, and the amount of time Gabrielle was likely to spend in the hospital.

Gabrielle knew the effects of treatment better than anyone and chose a regimen that Dr. deMontigny had explained would probably keep her feeling reasonably well for 12 to 18 months. But he had added, unless something miraculous happened, Gabrielle would probably not live much longer than that.

Yvette described a feeling of eerie half-normalcy in the months that followed. Gabrielle remained on the treatment and saw doctors regularly. They kept looking for any new experimental treatments for which Gabrielle might qualify, but none turned up.

As Dr. deMontigny had predicted, for almost a year and a half Gabrielle did reasonably well. She attended school most of the time, although she often lacked energy and the loss of hair kept her from feeling socially comfortable among her peers. Then, in the late fall, she developed non–Hodgkin's lymphoma, a second form of cancer that may have developed because her immune system was weakened by the leukemia treatment.

She and her family were camping at a lake on a family holiday when Gabrielle showed her mother a lymph node just behind and below her right ear. It was about the size of a small olive. Within two weeks it was the size of a small walnut. But it didn't hurt her at all. She and Yvette agreed they wouldn't tell Dr. deMontigny about it unless he noticed it. Yvette said, "We just didn't want to have to face reality."

As soon as Dr. deMontigny examined the node, it was biopsied. The new diagnosis was awful news. Gabrielle had to start on a couple of weeks of daily radiation therapy. She tolerated the treatment fairly well. But then her energy just gave out.

I asked Yvette if Gabrielle had ever talked to her about death.

"In November, after we got the diagnosis of the lymphoma, we were all pretty upset," Yvette responded. "That evening the house felt still, somber. I sat with Gabrielle in her room, on her bed. We talked for a long time. She was physically feeling okay at the time.

"'Will dying hurt?' she asked. 'I don't think so, darling,' I said. I promised her that her father and I would not let her hurt and that Dr. deMontigny had assured me that he would never let her suffer.

"'What will being dead be like?' she asked. 'Is there a life after death?' I told her that I didn't know, but I thought there was. I said, 'If there is life after death, you can be sure that your grandparents will be there waiting for you with open arms.' I have no doubt about that.

"I left her room that night and curled up in my husband's arms and cried and cried."

A Perfect Moment

By late November Gabrielle was spending most of her time on the couch. Adam and Yvette put a hospital bed in the living room so Gabrielle could be part of the action. A week later, fever and low blood counts required her to be readmitted to the cancer center for transfusions and antibiotics for a new infection. Yvette again stayed with her, sleeping at the Ronald McDonald House nearby.

Just after 4 A.M. one day, Gabrielle's fever spiked. Yvette called Adam and told him to come right away and then raced to the hospital. Gabrielle was moaning and incoherent. "I realized that the nurses were rushing," said Yvette. "They were in an emergency state, moving quickly, not trying to save her life, but to make things *quiet*. I went to the washroom and looked at myself in the mirror. 'This can't be the end,' I thought. 'I'm not ready!'

"It seems unbelievable, but, at this point, we were totally unprepared for Gabrielle to die. We had dealt with each step in her decline, but dying was always somewhere in the distant future. I finally realized that Gabrielle was dying, and that meant we needed to change our focus. When Adam arrived, I took him aside. 'I think we have to tell Gabrielle that it's okay for her to go,' I told him. 'We need to give her permission to die. I want to tell her how grateful we are for her.' Adam agreed, so we took her into our arms. I sat behind her in the bed and cradled her and Adam and I asked for her forgiveness."

That surprised me. "What for?" I asked.

"We had thought that she was going to get well, and

we'd been tough on her. She could be headstrong and defiant. She had so much talent and promise. Adam and I made
her take her schoolwork and responsibilities in the family
seriously. I think we overdid it. So we apologized.

"Adam said, 'Gaby, this illness was not your fault. You
did everything you could, and I'm so proud of you.'
Gabrielle had recently apologized to Adam for choosing
'the wrong treatment,' referring to her decision to go with
a treatment regimen that was less rigorous than others that
we had considered with Dr. deMontigny. It was heart-
wrenching. At the time, he had hugged her and told her it
wasn't her fault, but now Adam didn't want her to have any
lingering shred of doubt.

"We told her how thankful we were to have her for our
daughter and how much we loved her. We told her that she
was a gift to us from God. And we told her that we were
going to miss her, but that we would be okay. I told her
again, as I had that other night, that I felt her grandparents
would be there to greet her.

"It was an intense moment, a perfect moment. I can't
describe it. It was the worst thing—and yet it was the most
intimate and important time. I felt so grounded and connected. It felt right—as though we were finally down to
bedrock, living the basic truth of who we were to each
other and what our lives were about. That's what I felt with
the three of us there in the middle of the night in that little
bed. I remembered when Gabrielle was born and we both
held her in our arms, except now the love that Adam and I
shared was in her, and it was moving through all three of us
and enveloping us.

"We held her for the longest time. She slept, and I finally lay her back in bed and sat by her side. It was morning by now, and, to our amazement and joy, Gabrielle woke up. She smiled, 'I would really like some champagne and some Hershey's Kisses,' she said. And we all just started laughing and crying. She had just turned sixteen. She was brighter and stronger than she had been in days, maybe weeks. It was a miracle. To me it is still a miracle. It was utterly beautiful and incredibly sad."

Then Gabrielle announced she wanted to have her champagne and chocolate Kisses party at home. She wanted to see her brother and sister and the Christmas tree they had decorated. When they had described it to her over the phone a few days earlier, she'd told them she was certain they had not done it properly. Yvette and the nurses were not about to deny Gabrielle her wish, but going home was not a simple matter. She had IVs, injectable medicines, and oxygen that she needed just to live, and bedside equipment for her comfort and care. Luckily, one of the nurses was in her room when she asked and somehow they made it happen—the prescriptions, oxygen, hospital bed, paperwork, all of it.

Yvette said, "When we got home my sister-in-law, Claudette, was there. We had called ahead and she'd picked up the champagne and chocolate. Gaby's brother and little sister had set up a bed in front of the Christmas tree and Gaby settled in. We made a toast to her life and our family. She was grinning, lying there in front of the Christmas tree. She told her siblings it looked spectacular, and she ate some of the Kisses.

"Then, suddenly, she said she felt queasy. I went to the linen closet in the bathroom to get a fresh, damp face cloth. Gabrielle said to Claudette, 'Oh, my mother takes so much time.' I had just walked back and laid the cool cloth across her forehead when she looked out into the distance, almost as if she were surprised, took her last breath, closed her eyes, and died."

Yvette describes Gabrielle's last hours as a "perfect moment" and over the years I've thought a lot about what had made it perfect. When Yvette was finally able to accept the unacceptable—that her daughter was dying—it provided an opening into a realm of communication and connection with her daughter. She couldn't change what was; she could only shift her attitude. She chose to see Gabrielle as a gift. For the rest of the day, she did all she could to honor and celebrate her daughter's brief life.

Gabrielle understood that, too. Illness and impending death had made her wise beyond her years. When there was nothing left unsaid and Gabrielle and her parents had stopped denying her mortality, their remaining time together became a celebration.

Yvette remarked that the time she spent with Gabrielle during those final hours was strongly reminiscent of the time when Gabrielle was an infant. Mother and daughter would spend hours and hours staring at each other and cooing. Those last hours were exactly that—mother and daughter lost in a reverie of love for each other.

That kind of love is available to all of us. But to achieve it we must again become innocent. By this I mean that we must drop all preconceptions and pretense about ourselves and the world and freshly experience the wonder that is all around us. In so doing we are infused with the miracle of life, and we glow with amazement and awe. Every day is the first day of the world. By cracking open the shell of self-identity and laying us open to our essential selves, illness and impending death often force this fresh view of the world. This is what is meant by the expression "In dying we are newly born."

It happened naturally for Gabrielle and her parents—and I've seen it happen often with families when someone is dying. There is intense joy that comes to us and we want to celebrate the true miracle of our love for one another.

Every life is a full life. No one can tell us how long we will live or when we will die. The best strategy is to live each day as fully as possible. As if it were the first day, or the last day of your life. Each moment can then become perfect.

Gabrielle had it right: champagne and chocolate!

CHAPTER SEVENTEEN

Lives Intertwined with Love

It's hard to imagine how Lisa Oliver, whom you'll meet in this chapter, felt during the years that her sister, Linda, was living with breast cancer. It is an understatement to say that their relationship was very close and their lives were intertwined, or that they were not only sisters but best friends. Lisa and Linda were part of each other—they were identical twins.

Lisa used love as a way of coping with her sister's illness and dying. Her story reveals how each of us can practice love as a deliberate strategy for dealing with the pain of unacceptable loss. It requires practice to respond to anguish with love, but it works. Each time a wave of grief threatens to tear you apart, ask yourself, "What does love ask of me now?" How can you be more loving toward the person who is dying or has died, and to other important people in his or her life? How can you be more loving toward yourself?

Identical Genes

Lisa was born six minutes after Linda. She sometimes jokingly referred to Linda as my "older sister." As infants they were fed together, dressed together, and never more than a few feet apart. Their parents described how they would lie in their crib and stare at each other, giggling and mumbling baby talk. A photo of them at 10 months of age shows one is sucking the other's nose. To this day, no one knows which one was which.

They were inseparable through grade school and high school in rural, eastern Kansas. They shared an apartment at college in Lawrence; Lisa graduated with a business degree and Linda with a teaching certificate.

Through all those years, they never fought. They were so in tune that they could often finish each other's sentences. In a group of friends or on a double date, a nod or "a look" communicated all they needed to say. It didn't surprise anyone when both of them married men from the small community in which they'd grown up and settled down to raise families less than a 20-minute drive apart.

"Sometimes we would phone back and forth three times a day," said Lisa. "If Linda came to town for groceries, she'd often leave her kids with us for an hour. You can't get many groceries in a cart when you have two babies in tow."

Their family history was pockmarked by cancer—thyroid and colon cancer on their father's side, and breast cancer on their mother's. It was part of the genetic makeup they shared. They always knew they were at high risk for cancer, and they and their doctors checked for it frequently. When a lump under Linda's arm was biopsied and found to be breast cancer, it was hard to say who felt worse.

"I felt bad about feeling so bad!" Lisa recalled, smiling ruefully. "Linda kept comforting me by telling me I had a right to feel bad. She said we would get through this together."

And they did. Linda had bilateral mastectomies and was started on chemotherapy. Five months after her surgery—following lots of discussion with doctors and late nights reading on the Web—Lisa followed suit and had bilateral, prophylactic mastectomies and implant surgery.

Linda supported her sister in the decision. Her cancer had developed despite years of normal mammograms, annual physicals, and frequent self-exams. Given the twins' identical genetics, it was the prudent thing to do. It wasn't a symbolic act of solidarity with her sister—nor did she feel the need to shave her head in solidarity when Linda lost her hair from chemotherapy. Lisa's surgery, instead, was just another in a life-long succession of landmarks in a lifetime of shared experience. They had been gleeful together at the age of 10 when breast buds miraculously appeared. Now, at the age of 37, however sad, it seemed somehow natural to be losing their breasts together.

From the very beginning Lisa took Linda to doctors' appointments for chemo and for tests in Kansas City when Philip, her husband, had to work. They shopped together for Linda's wigs and breast prosthesis. Lisa attended the "Look Good, Feel Good" course with her sister and learned to administer medications through her central line.

She spent countless nights with Linda at the hospital, help-ing her bathe and massaging her back.

When Linda was in the hospital or just too ill, Lisa helped clean her home, cook meals, and plant her garden. She was the soccer mom for all four of their boys. Linda and Philip's boys stayed over, watched videos, and ate pizza with Lisa and her husband and sons.

Linda's cancer was relentlessly aggressive; within months it outsmarted each of the drugs the doctors used to combat it. She also had more complications from treatment than most patients. Two years after her diagnosis Linda devel-oped painful tumors in her ribs and spine. Radiation treat-ments cauterized the metastases and relieved her pain. But while she was in the hospital she developed a blood disor-der called thrombotic thrombocytopenic purpura or TTP. Her immune system started making abnormal proteins that caused her red blood cells and platelets to clot in her liver, spleen, and kidneys. This left her profoundly anemic and unable to form normal blood clots if she had the slightest injury.

"Every other day," said Lisa, "they would hook a ma-chine into a main vein in her neck and circulate her blood out and back in. Linda felt horrible. That was one time Linda said she just didn't want to do this anymore. Then a doctor told us that sometimes taking the spleen out would kick your system back in."

When plasmapheresis—in which a patient's blood is cir-culated through a machine that filters out proteins that are causing the blood cells to clump—fails, removing the spleen, which can be engorged with trapped blood cells, often controls the problem. It worked, but it took a while for Linda to get her strength back. Her weight had dropped to just 89 pounds.

For a time, things were relatively stable and life resumed a more normal pace, but about five years after her diagnosis, tumors in her liver began obstructing the flow of bile. Once again she was in the cancer center in Kansas City for weeks, separated from her family.

One day Linda abruptly announced that she was going to die and summoned her family to the hospital. It was a surreal scene. Linda was sitting up in her hospital bed with the sheets neatly tucked around her. The nurses had helped her fix her hair and makeup. It was a solemn event. She told each of her family members that she loved them. She said she was sorry for being so sick and sorry that she wouldn't be there for them. She told the boys how proud she was of them and that she was sure they were going to be great men.

Linda asked for a priest to give her the Sacrament of the Sick. "I don't know how to die," Linda said to him. "Can you help me?" He said he would pray for her to have a gentle passage into the arms of the Lord. The family all held hands and prayed. They were all crying, but Lisa noticed Linda didn't look as bad as she had a few weeks before: she had lots of energy.

In the morning, Linda was still alive, but she started saying strange things. She called Lisa at two in the morning the next night crying and said Phil was trying to poison her.

The doctors thought that Linda might have tumors in her brain, but a CT scan was clear. They concluded that

Decadron, a steroid medication they were giving her to shrink the tumors in her liver, was to blame.

"Everything they tried to make her better seemed to make things worse," said Lisa. "It was awful. She needed the steroids to control her tumors and they were making her crazy. The doctors were able to insert a tube through her side and drain the bile into a small bag she wore and then to wean her off the Decadron."

When Linda was finally tapered off the steroids and had her wits about her again, decisions about treatment had to be made. Linda was ready to give up. She told Lisa and Philip that she was fed up with being ill. Her doctor encouraged and Lisa and Philip pleaded with her to try one more round of chemotherapy. Without it she had little chance of living more than a few months. It took some doing, but she relented.

"That is the one thing I felt guilty for, for a long time," said Lisa. "She didn't want to take that last round of chemo. 'I can't take it,' she told us. 'I can't take anymore.' Philip and I talked her into it. I can picture myself trying to convince her, 'Oh, come on, Linda. This is the last one; this is the last one you have to take.'"

The chemotherapy worked. It shrank her tumors but also severely damaged her kidneys. That meant renal dialysis, three and a half hours three times a week at a center that was an hour and a half away. It also meant occasional surgeries to create or repair the arteriovenous shunts that were needed for dialysis. Life was not fun.

"Two years later," said Lisa, "when she really was dying,

if there was anything I needed to ask forgiveness for, it was that. We just couldn't bear the thought of her dying. She might have been ready years earlier, but we weren't."

Seeing her sister and best friend so ill would have been hard for any sibling. For Lisa, Linda's relentless consumption by her cancer was like looking in a ghostly mirror. "It was like having half of me die," said Lisa.

By the end, Linda's body had been ravaged by seven years of cancer and seven years of cancer treatment. After partially recovering a few months earlier, her kidneys had shut down again. Then her liver failed and she became confused and drifted into a coma. Her family doctor admitted her to the small, rural community hospital. Her family held a vigil there over the weekend.

"On Sunday I slept with her in her hospital bed," said Lisa. "I crawled in and slept until the nurses kicked me out at three in the morning because they had to turn her."

On Monday morning, Linda was still alive, and Lisa decided to go to work. At four o'clock a nurse called and told Lisa to come back to the hospital. Linda was showing signs of pneumonia and could die any moment.

Lisa raced to Linda's side. She was breathing hard and drooling. "Philip and I sat with her," said Lisa. "He cradled her back and I held her hand. She grunted a few times and just died. I remember how quiet and still it was. I think it was a long time until I could take a breath myself. I often wondered if I would die with Linda. I was almost surprised that I was still here. I felt so grateful to be with her at the end."

Lisa and Linda hadn't revisited the Four Things in any

formal way. "We knew what was on each other's hearts and we could read each other's minds," said Lisa. "She knew I was sorry for coercing her into having chemotherapy that time. And I knew she forgave me. The only thing I regret is that I wish I had said, 'I love you' more. She knew that I loved her, but I still wish I had said it more often. Linda did write me a couple of thank-you notes in the weeks before she died. I've kept them. The first one was when we returned from Disneyland, where we had gone with her boys. 'Thanks for including our sons in your family holiday!' she wrote. 'We really appreciate your kindness. They had a GREAT time. I hope they weren't too rambunctious. I love you!' The second one Linda gave me just a week before she died. It says, 'Thank you for no Geraniums! But thanks for always being there. Thank you for all the visits and encouragement. You are my guardian angel and best friend. I love you always.'"

Lisa told me there hasn't been an hour that goes by that she doesn't think of her sister. Two weeks after Linda died, Philip gave away all her clothes and sold her good china. Lisa was angry. "He didn't even think to ask if I wanted to keep them, maybe for my kids," she said. "Then he started dating. I think maybe it's a guy thing, a way of dealing with grief."

There's some truth in Lisa's comment. I've seen this response to grief in both sexes, but more often in men than women. Particularly after a protracted debilitating illness, it's as if the bereaved widower or widow has been grieving for so long that there is nothing left to grieve. Surviving spouses feel relieved and have an overpowering need to reinvest in life and the future. Does this reflect avoidance of pain on the part of the survivor? Maybe, but so what?

The sorrow that Lisa feels cannot be minimized. Part of her died with her sister. Yet she feels intact and whole, fully engaged in life and looking toward the future. And Linda will never really leave her. Lisa sees a bit of her sister each time she looks in the mirror. But it's a healthy Linda she sees, and a healthy Linda that she carries with her.

Henry David Thoreau wrote, "There is no remedy for love but to love more." Death makes us aware of the importance of the people we love and the sustaining force of love in our lives. When someone close to us is dying or has died, we can use love to burn through our grief and come to a place of gratitude for each other and for being alive.

PART FIVE

Good-bye

To every thing there is a season, and a time to every purpose under heaven: a time to be born and a time to die; a time to plant, and a time to pluck up that which is planted.

ECCLESIASTES

Introduction

Good-byes are the thing we dread most. In saying good-bye we acknowledge an inevitable separation. Yet life often becomes more precious (or, more accurately, the preciousness of life is often more clearly revealed) when we acknowledge our impermanence. If we are conscious of this impermanence as we say good-bye, each parting can remind us that our lives are precious.

By saying or conveying the essence of the Four Things, even painful farewells can contribute to the history and wholeness of love between two people. The Four Things can help us accept good-byes for what they are—an inevitable part of loving and a necessary part of full and healthy living!

As Ecclesiastes says, "To every thing there is a season. . . ." By saying good-bye in a conscious way, we offer the person we're parting with our blessing and give them the gift of our love.

When someone close to us is dying, the awareness of this impending, final parting can wrench our soul. When the Four Things have been said, however—or their essence conveyed—good-bye can also be bittersweet, accompanied by a deepening awareness of who we are—of what it means to be human.

Daniel Schumann reveled in life. An Ivy League education and success in business enabled him to travel the world and enjoy life to its fullest. When Daniel was forced to confront the end of his life at age 39, it would have been understandable for him to "rage against the dying of the light." For such an accomplished, vital man, saying good-bye might have seemed like a defeat. Daniel did not allow himself to get stuck in anger about things he couldn't change. Instead, he played the cards he'd been dealt as smartly as possible. Daniel wrote his mother this last letter, so that she would never doubt that he lived fully and joyfully through the very end of life, and that even though his death was premature, he was ready to say good-bye.

Dear Mom,

This last part of my life could have been very unpleasant, but it wasn't. In fact, in many ways, it has been the best part of my life. When you get down to it, I'd have to live several hundred years to fulfill all my dreams. I've done well with the time allotted me, so I have no regrets. I probably never would have slowed up enough to really ap-

preciate all of you if it hadn't been for my illness. That's the silver lining in this very dark cloud. I feel sorry for people who die not having had the chance to fulfill some of their dreams, as I have.

If anyone ever asks you if I went to heaven, tell them this: I just came from there.

Love, Daniel

Each life has a beginning, middle, and end. What's important is not how long but how deeply and fully we live. True enjoyment of life is not a passive experience: it's about deliberately investing one's life with joy. People who are dying have shown me that when we complete our relationships and celebrate the love that is at our core, we can realize Daniel's "heaven on earth."

Life presents us with a choice: we can choose to protect ourselves from emotional pain—or we can acknowledge our vulnerability and open ourselves to the loss that love will ultimately entail.

To love truly is inevitably to experience loss. We will die, and we will have to say good-bye to the people we love. We will have to leave them behind as we embark on that "journey from which no traveler returns." Or those we love will die first, and we will have to let them go and learn to live on without them. You may already have had to let go of people you've loved.

A Greek Orthodox priest I know pauses in every wedding ceremony he performs to remind those assembled that in bringing this couple and these families together in love and commitment, they will also be bound during times of illness, tragedy, and sadness. He does it in a way that does not destroy the joyfulness of the occasion, but deepens the day's celebration of life's fullness.

If we choose to protect ourselves from the pain of saying good-bye, never daring to love fully, we are only half alive. None of us wants that for ourselves or our children.

CHAPTER EIGHTEEN

Nothing Left Unsaid

Thankfully, not all stories end in loss, and not all good-byes directly precede death. Still, when a person we love is departing, we have a chance to complete our relationship by expressing forgiveness, appreciation, and love. Beyond an opportunity to "clear the air" or "clean the slate," when we part in the spirit of the Four Things, we acknowledge the preciousness of the other person and affirm the life and love we share.

Reverend and Mrs. Williams were able to say good-bye in this spirit to their son as he left to go to war in Iraq.

Dear Dr. Byock:

When my son left for the war in Iraq, we didn't know if we would ever see him again. Something I learned from you years ago helped my wife and I get through a very difficult time. . . .

Reverend Williams' letter touched me. I receive a lot of mail about the Four Things, but as a parent, I am particularly struck by the pain of a child going off to war.

Reverend Williams had heard me speak in the mid-nineties at a pastoral-care conference in Minneapolis. He had used the Four Things in his ministerial counseling ever since. And, he told me, he had used them before his son shipped out to the Middle East.

John Williams has been a preacher with a conservative congregation in Kentucky for the past 30 years. He organizes his life around the trinity of God, country, and family. He served as a Marine corps chaplain in Vietnam and saw the horrors of war firsthand. He believes the Vietnam war was a tragic political mistake, but his pride in America has never wavered, and he was proud when his son, Matthew, joined the service.

I called John immediately and arranged to have dinner with him and his wife, Betty, three weeks later when I was going to be speaking nearby in Lexington, Kentucky.

We met in the lobby of the Lexington Hilton. As soon as I saw him I remembered John from the conference. He was a large man with penetrating eyes and bushy salt-and-pepper eyebrows that contributed to a calm, distinguished presence. Betty was pretty and petite; her carefully considered words revealed her strength of character.

As soon as the waitress in the hotel restaurant left with our order, the Williams told me their story. In late fall 2002 Matthew was home from base for a brief visit before his unit of Marine Special Forces was deployed to the Persian Gulf.

Knowing that he would be gone over the holidays, they planned an early Christmas celebration and counted the days until his scheduled leave. Finally the doorbell rang, and there was Matthew, the youngest of their four children.

At 22, said John, Matthew was fully 3 inches taller than his father and 30 pounds lighter—a lean, muscular man.

"I remember wondering if he had finally stopped growing," said his mother with a quiet laugh.

"We try not to gush," said John, "because it makes Matthew uncomfortable, but we well up with pride each time we look at him."

Matthew's decision to enlist after high school had been the right one because at 18 Matthew wasn't ready for college. Though he was bright and good natured, he had gotten into trouble a few times during his teens—nothing too serious, the sort of pranks (stealing the opposing team's jerseys during March Madness one year, for example) that come with an excess of testosterone. It was a scandal because he was a minister's son. The military's training and discipline had accelerated his maturation.

Except for dinners and, of course, church services, they saw little of Matthew during his three-day leave. He spent most of his time with friends, especially Sara Ann, his first real girlfriend.

Betty said, "We are very fond of Sara Ann. That weekend I asked Matthew how serious he was about their relationship. He said, 'Mom, I love her, but I couldn't ask her to marry me now.' He meant that he couldn't ask her to make that kind of commitment to him, knowing that he might not come back from the war. He didn't want to risk leaving her as a young widow. I thought to myself, that is real love."

Despite the festive atmosphere, the Williams recognized the nature of Matthew's visit and before he left, they met in the reverend's study.

Reverend Williams began by telling his son how very proud he was of the man he had become. He asked his forgiveness for the words of anger that had passed between them during the times they had fought when Matthew was in high school, and told his son that he forgave him for those years of mischief. "I told him that I recognized that he had grown up: I could see it in the way he held himself. Then I told him how thankful we were to God for giving Matthew to us. I said, 'Matthew, thank you for being such a wonderful son. I love you very much.'"

"Wow, you really do practice what you preach," I said. "What an incredible gift that must have been for Matthew. How did he respond?"

"Matthew was more solemn than we had ever seen him," said John. "He told us that he loved us and apologized for the trouble he had caused. He said how much he appreciated our patience with him and our guidance. He said that he had grown in the last two years, that 9/11 made him realize that his own family and friends were in danger. He felt his Marine training and service gave him a way to do something about that danger."

I nodded. "Because of your experience in Vietnam," I said, "you knew all too well the sort of dangers that he would face. Did you advise him?"

"I told him that the military is a team effort. I asked him

to please be as safe as possible and not take unnecessary risks. I reminded him to pray frequently, and I said that Jesus would watch over him."

Betty added, "And we told him that we would be praying for him many times a day."

"Was there anything else that you said to him, Mrs. Williams?" I asked.

"I said, 'I am so proud of you! It's so hard to see you go. As big as you are, you've been my baby. Now, I realize I can't protect you anymore.'"

"How did he respond?"

"'Mom,' he said. 'Maybe this is my time to protect you!'"

A Heart Outside the Body

It's been said that the decision to have children is a decision to have your heart walk around outside your body. I asked the Williams what it was like watching the war in real time on television. They were grateful for the constant coverage, but it was both a blessing and a curse. They were glued to the news, following the movements of Matthew's unit as closely as possible. Every time a reporter mentioned that the Marine Special Forces "were meeting resistance" John and Betty knew it meant someone was shooting at their son!

I thought about the Williams many times over the next months. I shuddered to imagine what it must be like to have one's child in a war zone, "in harm's way." During the invasion of Iraq I found myself scanning the newspaper's list of fallen American soldiers for Matthew Williams, always relieved when his name wasn't there.

I called the Williams after the intense phase of fighting in Iraq had subsided and asked if they had heard from their son. It turned out that Matthew was back in the United States. He had been wounded in a helicopter accident in Northern Iraq, but was almost fully recovered. He had told his parents that after completing his commitment to the military, he planned to start college. He and Sara Ann were talking about getting married.

I asked the Williams how their meeting in the study with Matthew had affected them when they were told that he was wounded.

Betty spoke for both of them. "I already had the experience of waiting for one man to come home from the war," she said, referring to John. "When he was away, I had a long time to think about the worst that could happen. With Matthew leaving to fight for his country, it was a comfort for us to know that if the worst happened—if he were captured, or wounded and did not survive—our son would know how thoroughly we loved him. He would have no worries that there was anything left unsaid."

It needn't take a war or terrorist attacks for us to realize how precarious life is. We are all at risk of dying suddenly from a car crash or heart attack. Epidemics such as West Nile virus and SARS can cause perfectly healthy people who were doing perfectly normal things to sicken and die within days. It could happen to you or me.

The fact that any of us—and any of the people we love—could die at any time serves as a constant reminder to keep our relationships current. "Your life dwells among the causes of death/Like a lamp standing in a strong breeze." The Dalai Lama, in his book *Advice on Dying*, quotes Nagarjuna's *Precious Garland*. Death is all around us and could come at any moment.

Are there people in your life about whom, were they to die suddenly, you would worry that you had left important things unsaid? If tomorrow a person you love was suddenly confined to an Intensive Care Unit isolation bed, awake but unable to breathe without a ventilator and unable to speak, would he or she worry about things left unsaid between the two of you? If so, today is a good day to make the Four Things explicit.

CHAPTER NINETEEN

The Mysterious Magic of Some Good-byes

In the field of hospice and palliative care, we often care for people who, it seems, delay their death in order to achieve some goal, such as attending a wedding, holding a new grandchild, or completing a life-long relationship. Those of us who work with people who are dying see this all the time.

Critics have long dismissed such notions as myth. Scientific colleagues, citing sound physiologic facts, point out how improbable it is that a patient who is dying of cancer, heart failure, or stroke could exert any influence over the timing of his or her demise.

Recent scientific studies, however, have backed up what we in the field have known from experience—that people can postpone their own deaths to be present for a signifi-

cant social event, perhaps to say good-bye. Dr. David
Phillips and associates at the University of California in San
Diego saw a significant statistical dip in the number of
deaths just before holidays such as Passover and the Chi-
nese Harvest Moon Festival, followed by a rise in deaths
the week after these holidays. This pattern recurs each year,
but only among the ethnic groups for which these occasions have special meaning. The only plausible explanation
for this finding is that people have postponed their inevitable departure for one final celebration with family and
friends.

Thirty-five-year-old Sandy Cummings, a beloved husband and son, died suddenly, but mysteriously remained in
physiologic limbo until the people who loved him were
ready to say their final farewells.

Staying Around to Say Good-bye

Sandy suffered sudden cardiac arrest, and, when his heart
was restarted, he entered a persistent vegetative state.
Nothing in medical science suggested why Sandy's heart
should have stopped suddenly and I still don't know why
Sandy didn't finish dying while his heart was in arrest.

I will never forget the way in which Sandy's family—it
seems with his help—reached closure and found peace before Sandy let go of life.

Before Sandy collapsed, he was vibrantly healthy, a non-
smoker with no family history of heart disease and no
known health problems. He worked as a commercial fisher-

man in the summer and a forestry surveyor in the spring and fall and was exceptionally fit.

Seconds after Sandy collapsed in Missoula while waiting to bowl his fourth frame during a regional tournament, bystanders began CPR and called 911. He was rushed to a hospital where, with drugs and electrical shock, his heart was restarted.

At the hospital early the next morning, Ann Cummings found her husband in an eerie state between life and lifelessness. Although he was breathing normally and reflexively opened his eyes to loud noises, the EEG tracing of brainwaves from his cerebral cortex (the thinking "gray matter" part of the human brain) was a flat line. This most sophisticated outer layer of the brain is farthest from arteries carrying oxygen-rich blood, and the more primitive, central, and basal parts of the brain are more resilient to lapses in circulation.

Dr. Lucas, the neurologist, explained to Ann that when Sandy's heart stopped, his cerebral cortex had died. The brain scan, MRI, and repeated EEG tests confirmed this. Sandy's brainstem was still regulating his breathing, temperature, and other autonomic functions and causing reflex responses, which is why his eyes opened in response to noise, but there was no evidence of consciousness: any awareness or capacity to think. In such situations recovery is extremely rare, but if there were a chance that Sandy would recover they would see a change in his condition within a few days.

Dr. Lucas counseled Ann, "Well-meaning friends will tell you about miraculous recoveries from comas. Although

I have never personally seen someone awaken from a prolonged coma, it is true that miracles sometimes occur, but it is also true in such cases that the person is always profoundly damaged, mentally and physically. I am not prejudging the value that such a life would hold for you or Sandy; I only want you to have all the facts." He waited for the weight of his words to settle, before continuing. "I'm sorry. I wish I could paint a brighter picture."

Ann summoned the courage to telephone Sandy's parents, Thomas and Lucille, to tell them what had happened. "I need you more than anything," she said. "Please come." They caught the first plane from Massachusetts.

Although Ann had gently warned her parents-in-law what to expect, they gasped when they entered Sandy's room. It wasn't Sandy, but a ghostly apparition of their son. Thomas shook his head and observed sadly, without humor, "The lights are on, but nobody's home."

After a week of watching her husband linger in this limbo and avoiding the subject, Ann told her in-laws that Sandy would not want to exist like this. For his sake, to honor what she knew would have been his wishes, she wanted to talk to the doctor about withdrawing Sandy's life-support systems. She was his spouse and legal proxy, but Ann wanted her in-laws' advice and consent. "He's my spouse, but he's your child," she told them. They shared her bleak realism and assessment of Sandy's wishes.

As the family instructed, the doctors took Sandy off artificial life-support systems, issued a "Do Not Resuscitate" order, and gradually weaned him from his ventilator. He didn't die suddenly. His brainstem continued to act as coxswain to his vigorous body, calling out the physiologic rhythms. After a few days, a "PEG tube" (for percutaneous endoscopic gastrostomy) was inserted through the skin of his abdomen to drip nutrient formula into his small intestine. This too was a form of medical life support, yet it seemed prudent to both the doctors and Ann to maintain Sandy's body in this way, while watching closely for any sign of improvement.

Ann and his parents spent day after day at the hospital. Then Sandy was moved to a nursing home where Ann sat beside him for two weeks, talking quietly, reading to him, or just being there.

As the ordeal progressed, Ann and the Cummings discovered qualities in one another that they had never known and forged bonds that would last a lifetime.

Finally, after nearly a month without any improvement, Ann asked Sandy's doctor to discontinue the artificial nutrition and hydration that were sustaining his body. This is an ethically acceptable and entirely reasonable choice, but it is always a difficult decision. Ann drew strength from knowing beyond doubt that her husband would not have wanted to be kept alive in his condition by medical means. And it helped Ann that Sandy's parents agreed and supported her in honoring their son's wishes.

At the time, I was the hospice medical director for Missoula and Sandy's physician asked me to evaluate Sandy, to meet Ann and his parents, and offer my support. I wanted them to know we were doing everything possible to ensure Sandy's comfort. It was late afternoon when I visited them at the nursing home. Sandy had been in a coma for more than five weeks. Ann was as emotionally prepared for his inevitable death as she could be. She had spent countless hours at his bedside and, she assured me, had said her good-byes to him. She was somber but composed. We spoke for about 20 minutes before Ann left to go home for the evening.

I went to the nursing station, reviewed Sandy's chart, and spoke with the head nurse. As I reentered his room, Sandy was alone. I measured his vital signs, examined him, and confirmed the presence of only rudimentary neurologic reflexes. I noted his strong heartbeat, normal blood pressure, moist skin, and adequate urine flow.

I sat at Sandy's bedside and wrote in his medical chart my clinical impression that his body would probably live for another week. His parents came in, and I introduced myself and told them I had just examined their son. I expressed my regrets about their son's sudden, tragic illness and impending death.

"Is there anything else you can think of that I or any of us can do for Sandy, or to support you in this difficult time?" I asked.

Thomas Cummings, a slight, mild-mannered man in his late sixties, looked me straight in the eye and said, "Yes, but you probably won't do what I would ask you to do."

I held his gaze and replied, "Please tell me what that is."

I had a good idea what was coming, but it was important not to jump to conclusions. This was one of those situations in which it is crucial for people to say what's on their mind—and for me, as a doctor, to hear them out.

•   •   •

"Well, I'd want you to get this over with as soon as possible, for Sandy's sake," Mr. Cummings said firmly.

"You mean you want me to do something to end his life?"

"Yes," he replied.

This is no longer an unusual request from a patient's family. I recognize the depth of frustration and despair from which it arises. Death is inevitable, but their loved one's lingering seems meaningless and without value. However, allowing death to come is one thing. Administering a lethal injection is quite another: it is outside both my ethical and legal authority as a physician. Still, the suffering not only of a patient, but also of a patient's family, demands my attention.

"I hear what you are saying, sir," I said to Mr. Cummings. "It's hard to imagine how painful this must be for you. I can't fathom why Sandy is still here. But my role in this mystery doesn't include intentionally ending life, even now. I promise you that I won't do anything to prolong his dying, and I will do everything to make sure he is cared for meticulously and with dignity."

As I acknowledged the apparent meaninglessness of Sandy's coma, Mr. Cummings' eyes watered and he clenched his jaw as he tried to rein in the sadness that swept through him.

"Is it possible that he is hanging on for some reason?" I was grasping at therapeutic straws; I wanted to see if they could identify anything at all that held meaning or value for them during this time. "Was there anything that would have been left undone if he had died suddenly that night at the bowling alley?"

"It has been quite a couple of weeks," he admitted. "Coming here and meeting all of his friends, and spending time with Sandy and with Ann. As hard as this is, it would have been so much harder for both of us if he had gone suddenly. We've had the chance to tell him we love him. We only wish we could have known him better. In the last two weeks I've heard stories from Ann and his friends that have made me see my son in a different way. I think I understand him now, and that wasn't always true. I am so sorry that didn't happen sooner."

Mrs. Cummings chimed in. "We have come to know Ann and see her strength, and love her even more than we did. And we've come to appreciate just how much she loved Sandy—and"—she chuckled—"how much she put up with."

I assured them that Sandy's injury prevented any physical discomfort, but I would come back the next day and check on him. Driving home took about 10 minutes, and as I walked in the door, the phone rang. It was the nursing home, telling me that Sandy Cummings had just died.

The timing of Sandy's death startled me, coming so soon after Thomas Cummings had acknowledged the value of his son's lingering and that his family had had a chance to say good-bye and ease into their grief, particularly given my physical assessment just minutes before.

I could not avoid the impression that Sandy had been hovering at death's doorway to give everyone a little time to do what they needed before he finally left. Picturing my meeting with his parents, I envisioned Sandy's ethereal self in the room, knowing he couldn't return to life, but waiting for some assurance that his mother and father were truly ready for him to finish leaving. Everyone involved that day has wondered whether Thomas and Lucille's acknowledgment of their love for him and Ann, and the declaration of their strength as a family, was what allowed Sandy to let go.

I know that I do not know. In my work with people who are dying, I often feel that I stand with them on the threshold of the great mystery of time without end. I do not pretend to have answers. It is not within my capacity to discern ultimate meaning of life in the universe. I can only honor the mystery and hope to be of some service to others.

One thing is certain: experiences like that of Sandy Cummings and his family need not be understood on all levels for the power of their lessons to be felt. In addition to tragedy, a person's illness and dying have the capacity to burn and shake, and, ultimately, to transform anyone willing to stand close to it.

CHAPTER TWENTY

Good-byes That Are Gifts Through Time

Sometimes the good-byes we say need to last a lifetime. There are many ways to say good-bye and ensure that your love is received even if you're no longer alive.

If you are a parent who may be leaving young children behind, it is wise to assure them of your unconditional love and to wish them well in their own journey through life. Overly specific instructions and advice are prone to cause resentment in the years ahead. The world is changing rapidly. The world they will live in is impossible to anticipate, but will certainly be different from anything we now know.

Historically, a person's last will and testament, in addition to dividing property among heirs, included messages of love as well as carefully chosen pieces of parental guidance, advice, admonitions, and wisdom. Some people still use wills for this purpose, but, from what I've observed, the material expectations surrounding inheritance can seriously complicate family dynamics and even the most loving of messages can be misconstrued. It is probably better to use a separate vehicle—a letter or a videotape or messages of some sort to be opened on special days like birthdays, graduations, or weddings—to express the Four Things. By doing this we can project the loving sense of farewell (from *fare thee well*) that conveys the original blessing of good-bye or "God be with you" into the future. This was what Susan Armstrong, the 42-year-old woman with ALS whom you met earlier, was able to do.

Susan was losing all she loved in the world. Dying was immensely difficult for her, but Susan's sense of responsibility to those she loved was even deeper than her own pain. Although the disease robbed her of voice and breath, she was determined to honor her wedding vows, which, to her, meant letting go of and saying good-bye to the man she loved.

A Wedding Ring

Before the ALS and her medications made any communication with Susan impossible, she had not been eating or drinking for a week. Although death was not imminent, she was rapidly weakening. Under doctor's orders, her family was giving her small doses of morphine to ease her muscle pains. She would sleep off and on, but was not giving in to the drugs because she was waiting for her stepsister from out of state to visit. She was also hanging on for the "surprise" birthday party that her soon-to-be seven-year-old daughter, Allison, had been planning.

Susan had needed an alphabet board to communicate for several months; at this point in her illness, she became exhausted after spelling out a couple of words.

About a week before she would die, Richard was sitting next to Susan, simply spending time together as they often did, when she started weakly picking at her wedding ring. It was only a slightest twitch of her finger, but it represented an enormous effort, since she could barely move her fingers. Richard asked if the ring was hurting her. She gestured no with her eyes. He asked if it was slipping off because she was so thin. Again, she gestured no. Weakly, but insistently, she picked at the ring. When Richard asked if she wanted him to do something about it, she signaled yes. Confused, he asked if she wanted the ring off; she blinked yes. After Richard took it off her hand, she weakly pointed with her eyes toward his hand. "Are you asking me to take it?" Richard said, and her eyes told him yes.

A Vow Completed

Richard recalled his bolt of fear. Every imaginable anxiety crossed his mind. Uncertainly, he said, "I can think of many reasons why you might give this to me. You could be mad at me, or you could be saying good-bye." Because she could only answer yes or no questions, he continued: "Does this mean you are saying good-bye?" She blinked yes. Richard said, "Are you saying that you're ready to die?" Again, she blinked yes.

Richard and Susan had always been openly affectionate toward each other. He knew that his wife's return of her wedding ring was meant as a gesture of love. She was giving him the freedom to go on and fall in love again. He described how, following her gesture, the waning days of Susan's life were filled with caresses, kisses, words, and songs—every imaginable expression of the intensity and joy of their love.

For now, Richard wears both wedding rings. They are a sign for Allison of his undying love for her mother. Some day, he'll put them both away together in a treasured place, like the lasting memory of a marriage that was lovingly completed.

Susan also thought long and hard about a way to say good-bye to her six-year-old daughter that would also acknowledge and nurture their life-long relationship. With the help of four close friends, as her disease progressed Susan made gifts and dictated messages for Allison to open at every birthday through the age of 20 and at major life events. These gifts and the messages they contain remain wrapped, awaiting birthdays, graduations, and a wedding that Susan will never see.

Her first card for Allison began, "Dear Smoochie-girl, I hope your seventh birthday is terrific. I hope you have the best party ever. Don't forget how much I love you and that I am with you in spirit always. I did not want to leave you. You will always be my little girl and I will always be your

Mommy. I love you and Daddy so much. Happy birthday, Sweetie, love. Mommy."

Susan also picked out two books for Allison and a blank journal for her to write her thoughts. The first book was *The Next Place*, a wonderful kids' book with gorgeous illustrations, without a particular religious orientation. It is inscribed, "Happy 7th birthday Smoochie-girl. I love you so much, Mommy."

The other was a book called *Momma, Do You Love Me?* That one is inscribed, "Dear Allison, no matter where I am I will always be your Mom. Happy birthday, my beloved daughter. I love you forever." Allison has all these words from her mother, written in the hand of close friends.

Living Fully Through to the End

Although fate would not allow her to be there in real time, Susan realized that through her gifts and messages she could project her caring and affection into the future. In this way she could provide Allison with a measure of motherly love and affirmation during the formative years and critical events of her young life. Susan hoped her preparation would ease her family's pain at her premature death and reluctant good-bye. In taking care of her husband and daughter in this way, she was also taking care of herself. The project gave meaning to her days and, ever so slightly, eased her own grief at the impending loss they shared.

Susan said good-bye in a conscious way, turning her parting into a gift for the people closest to her that she was leaving behind. She blessed them with her love and made them feel that she was with them even when she was no longer physically present. Even when Susan was gone, she lived on inside her daughter, and her gifts to her child are reminders to us that some good-byes can last a lifetime.

CHAPTER TWENTY-ONE

Good-byes That Celebrate Life

Memorial services are often called celebrations of the life of the person who has died. When I was young, I thought this was a pointless attempt to paint over grief with platitudes, but in teaching and practicing the Four Things I've come to understand the importance of celebration. I've observed that among relatives and close friends, when there is nothing more to do or say, "celebration happens." People naturally, almost inevitably, celebrate their relationship and love for one another. People who are dying have taught me that we don't have to wait until a wake or memorial service to do this. We don't, in fact, have to wait until we're dying. Celebrations are more fun when the person being celebrated is present.

If You Need Me

Jessie works in the pharmacy at the Community Medical Center in Missoula, and her husband, Harold, teaches at the University of Montana. I bumped into them at our local Farmer's Market, which is held on Saturday mornings during the summer, and they said that they wanted to tell me a story. We sat in the shade, sipping coffee and munching fresh pastries.

Rose, Jessie's mother, had lived alone in Michigan and visited Missoula at least once a year for four weeks. Jessie was her youngest child. They had always been close, and had grown closer over the years. Rose loved Harold and her grandchildren, and she had fallen in love with Montana.

Jessie and her family looked forward to Rose's visits as much as Rose did. Through her eighties, Rose was active and intellectually alive. Her bedside table was stocked with Book-of-the-Month Club selections. When she was in Missoula she animatedly took part in dinners with their friends, and Jessie and Harold's friends became her friends as well.

A few years earlier, at 89, Rose fell and broke her hip and required months of rehabilitation. That year Jessie suggested that she and Harold would go to Michigan for their visit, but Rose wouldn't hear of it, refusing to miss her annual trip to Missoula. Rose usually came in early October after the university was in session and things had settled down for Jessie's household. So Jessie was surprised when, the week before Labor Day, her mother called and announced that she would arrive in Missoula in four days.

"She didn't say she was ill or anything was wrong,"

Jessie said. "She just said, 'I want to see Missoula one more time.' It was our running joke. But she did say one thing that gave me pause. She wanted to attend the Spirit of Peace Church 'one last time.' The way she said it gave me a lump in my throat."

Rose's granddaughter, Heidi, had always been incredibly close to Rose. That September, Heidi had been due to start college in Spain, but when she got there in mid-August she hated it and pleaded to come back to Missoula and enroll in the university. Harold and Jessie resisted. Heidi had made a commitment, and they thought she could still get something out of studying overseas. But when they told her Rose was coming early, she used it as leverage, and her parents reluctantly gave in.

Jessie said, "When Mom heard that Heidi was coming home, she didn't seem surprised. 'I never wanted her to go away to begin with,' she said. In retrospect, I wonder if they hadn't in some way colluded. When Mom called to announce she was coming, she said to me, 'If you are disappointed in all these changes of plans, that's too bad. This is what *I* want.' She had always been a real character, but she had never been pushy in quite that way. I put it down to being ninety-three."

Rose had to change planes twice, but she made the eight-hour trip to Missoula intact. She was very tired and needed to sleep. But the family had a few rituals she loved that had evolved over the years. She shared a beer with Harold in a frosted stein. After drinking half of it, she looked at him and said, "It doesn't taste very good, does it?" which he thought was odd.

Jessie bundled up her mother in front of the fireplace because she was cold, and manicured Rose's fingernails. Then she put her mother to bed.

The next day Rose was in great spirits. Harold and Jessie's barbecue lasted all afternoon as friends dropped by to welcome Rose back to town. That evening, Rose was exhausted. Jessie heard her moaning in the guest bathroom upstairs and called through the door to ask if she was all right.

"Mom said, 'I don't know, I have to go to the bathroom, but I can't, and I have to vomit but I can't.' When she came out I helped her to bed and I said: 'Mom, I'm going to stay here with you. That way, if you need to get up in the middle of the night I'll be here. We don't want you falling down.' 'Good idea,' she said. Frankly, it shocked me that she acquiesced. I had expected a fight."

The night was uneventful, and Rose rallied in the morning. It was the Tuesday after Labor Day, and the house was bustling. Harold made Rose a cup of tea before he left for work. Soon after, Jessie heard her mother in the bathroom throwing up. But that didn't relieve Rose's discomfort. When Jessie called her doctor, the office nurse told her to take her mother to an urgent care clinic. Harold rushed home from work. Rose was so weak that they had to carry her down the stairs.

"She was like a dried leaf," said Jessie. "She weighed next to nothing."

At the clinic, Rose had waves of terrible pain, "labor pains," she called them. The doctor listened to her symptoms, examined her, and told Harold and Jessie to take Rose to the emergency room. Later in the hall, the doctor added, privately to Jessie, "These little ones, you know, if they get dehydrated they can slip away really fast."

Each day we need to replace the fluid that evaporates from our skin and our breath. Like infants, frail elderly people can quickly become dehydrated from vomiting and being unable to drink. They often don't tolerate the loss of fluid and can suffer kidney failure, heart attacks, or strokes.

The doctor called ahead, and the emergency department was expecting Jessie and her mother when they arrived.

"Where I Need to Be"

On the way to the hospital, Rose was in pain, but she was alert and entirely clear. She asked Jessie which hospital they were taking her to. When Jessie said, "St. Patrick's," Rose brightened. "Oh, my God, really?" said Rose. "Well then, that's fine!'

"My mother was Irish Catholic," said Jessie. "So this was a good omen. She was a woman who believed in signs."

At the hospital Rose was given intravenous fluids, pain medication, and a battery of tests. A surgeon reviewed the X rays, which showed that Rose had a bowel obstruction from an "incarcerated paraesophageal hernia." Part of her stomach and small intestine had slipped through the diaphragm, alongside her esophagus, and become trapped in her chest.

The surgeon was patient and personable. He sat at Rose's bedside, and, as sensitively as he could, delivered the bad news and laid out two bad options. He could operate, but he told Rose that she was unlikely to survive, given the extent of the surgery involved, her age, and her generally frail condition. He added that if she did survive, she would have a colostomy and would most likely no longer be independent. The alternative was to treat her symptoms, make her comfortable, and "let nature take its course," a euphemism for saying that Rose would die over the next few days as bacteria and toxins from the herniated segment of her intestine gradually overwhelmed her system.

Jessie remembered his words. "'I'm trained to operate and I'm ready to do so,' he had said. 'But operations are not always the right decision. Everybody dies from something.'

"He said he'd support us in either choice," said Jessie. "But I could tell he was thinking, 'If this were my mother, I wouldn't put her through an operation.'"

Rose decided—it was her time. She was ready to go.

Jessie and Harold weren't surprised. Earlier that year, Rose had moved to Columbus, Ohio, for several months to care for her dying sister, Alice. After Alice died, Rose made out a power of attorney for health care documents, naming Jessie as her proxy if she couldn't speak for herself, and instructing Jessie that she was not to be kept alive if she couldn't respond. She had been explicit. She didn't want CPR, antibiotics, or tube feeding.

The doctor and nurses made Rose comfortable. Jessie and Harold called Heidi, Jessie's sisters, and Rose's other grandchildren to tell them what was happening. They called their friends who had become Rose's friends as well.

Rose settled into a private hospital room with a view of Lolo Peak in the distance. Medication made her groggy. But she was comfortable, at least most of the time.

"I opened the windows," said Jessie. "My mother looked at the mountains and said, 'Tell me the name of the hospital again.' 'St. Patrick's,' I answered. And again, she glowed. 'That's right,' she said as if this was the clincher, the final validation. 'I am where I need to be.'"

Lifted by Love

People and flowers started arriving at Rose's bedside, and, by evening, the place looked like the winners circle at the Kentucky Derby. Two couples from the Spirit of Peace Church came by and asked if they could say a prayer. Rose pulled herself together, sat up, and assumed the role of hostess, presiding over the affair.

"She held court," Harold said. "She was the queen bee."

Except for being set in a hospital and the fact that the guest of honor happened to be dying, the scene could have been a graduation party with people coming to express their love and well wishes, visiting briefly, and then saying good-bye so that others could do the same. The phone started ringing. Jessie, Harold, or Heidi spoke to the callers and relayed their words to Rose.

Jessie laughed as she reprised her role as master of ceremonies, "I'd pick up the phone and it would be one of the grandkids. 'Tell Grandma I love her,' he'd say. 'Tell her everything is going to be fine. Tell her we are praying for her, tell her we are sending her flowers.' I'd hang up and say, 'Mom, Jeffrey just called and he said to tell you that he loves you, he just adores you, and everything is going to be fine.' And Mom would say, 'Oh, God bless that Jeffrey.' And then it would be Maureen, and I'd say, 'Ma, that was Maureen on the phone. She said that she loves you so much.' And she'd say, 'God bless that Maureen.' Mom felt surrounded by everyone and lifted up by their love."

As the evening wore on, Rose lost her little remaining energy and gradually withdrew from the festivities.

Jessie, Harold, and Rose had some quiet, serious moments together. She told them that she loved them and thanked them for putting up with her all these years.

I asked if there were any expressions of regret or forgiveness.

Harold smiled, "Yes, she said she was sorry for imposing on us and hoped we'd forgive her. Then she almost smirked and said, 'But it sure was a good thing I came, wasn't it? I got to see Heidi. And I got to see Missoula again. I wanted to get to Spirit of Peace one last time, but it feels like I was there in spirit during the prayer this afternoon.'"

"Just Whisper"

Rose rested, fitfully at first, between intermittent spasms of pain and vomiting, before she gradually gave in to the medication. Jessie lay on a cot next to her.

"Before she fell asleep I said to her, 'I'm going to be right here, Mom. You know how much I love you. I'm right here. If you need me in the night, you just whisper.' 'I know that,' my mother said. 'I know you're right there. I'm fine.'"

Rose went to sleep but, in the middle of the night, her breathing changed. Jessie said Rose "rasped, as though there was phlegm deep in her chest."

Occasionally, toward morning, Rose would open her eyes and reach up as if "expecting to grasp someone's hand."

"It was as if she was in a waking dream," Jessie recalled. "At first, I thought she wanted something. I didn't know what. I put a rosary in her hand. She threw it across the room." Jessie laughed, "So that wasn't it. We couldn't figure out what her hand movements meant. At one point, when she was alert, I asked her. 'Alice is waiting for me,' she said, 'and your father and Grandpa Hughes.' 'Do you think that they are close because they are going to help you make this transition?' I asked. 'Absolutely,' she said. And she talked about the visit she'd just had with Alice.

"I thanked Mom for coming to be with us during this time. And she just looked at me and said 'I love you, sweetheart.'"

An Incredible Gift

By the time Jessie's sisters, Chris and Wendy, arrived, Rose seemed to be spending more time in the "next life" than in this one. Except for the occasional wave of vomiting, she slept, sometimes mumbling incoherently. But when Jessie's sisters entered the hospital room and kissed Rose, she somehow pulled herself back into the present, sat up, and greeted them.

"I'm so glad all my children are here," Rose said. "Now we can have a tea party!"

By the time the tea came and was served all around, Rose had drifted off again.

While their mother slept, Jessie's sisters checked in at the motel and the surgeon examined Rose. She wasn't in pain, but every time he touched her she would startle, as if roused from a dream.

"We were talking with him in the hall outside her room," Jessie said, "when I noticed she was trying to sit up, as if she needed to vomit. We went to her bedside and helped her sit, the doctor on one side and me on the other, and he said to me, 'Your mother has passed.' 'What?' I said. But then I looked at her and she was gone. I had never been so close to death before, but it wasn't eerie. She was luminous, and I was astonished. I thought, 'My God, this is like giving birth to a child.'"

Harold continued. "Chris and Wendy flew back to Michigan two days later. Rose's parish had arranged for a mass to be said in her honor that weekend. We were supposed to follow, bringing Rose's ashes with us. But then the September eleventh attacks occurred and we couldn't travel. So they had the mass without her ashes. And she got her wish to attend Spirit of Peace one last time—in an urn."

"What made you think that she had somehow arranged it all?" I asked.

"When we got to Michigan a few weeks later," Harold said, "we heard from one of Rose's friends and from a woman who looked in on her every day, that she had been having occasional bouts of pain and vomiting. She hadn't seen a doctor and they had never lasted long, but maybe she had an inkling that the condition was serious."

Jessie interrupted, "The other reason is that Wendy called while we were still in Missoula to say that while cleaning Mom's apartment she came across a copy of *Dying Well* on her dresser. It had been one of our book club books the year before and she had taken it home with her after a visit. Rose had gone through it, underlined lots of passages, made notes in the margins, and turned back a dozen or more pages. There were asterisks next to, *Please forgive me, I forgive you, Thank you, I love you, and Good-bye.* Wendy said that it made her think Mom had orchestrated the whole thing.

"She couldn't have *known* she was dying—but we're pretty certain she suspected it. She didn't want to see her doctor because if he found something she was afraid that he wouldn't let her travel. She didn't want to be marooned in Michigan. We didn't know it at the time, but she came here to die. I'm convinced it was her choice. What an incredible gift she gave us. She allowed me to shower her with care and affection in a way that will always remain precious to me. Her death was a transformative experience for the whole family. It was as if she had engineered it in a very practical, premeditated way!"

Rose's last visit and death also affected Heidi. It matured her and she grew inwardly. Her parents were proud of how present and loving she was in Rose's final hours and then after her death. She was a great comfort to Jessie. As Jessie was losing her last parent, she realized that she would be next; her generation was replacing the generation that came before it.

Jessie was thinking about this as she walked with her daughter back to their car after the funeral, and thinking what a lovely young woman she was. "I'm so glad you're here with me and not in Spain," Jessie said to her. Heidi smiled, a secret little smile. "I love you, Mom," she replied. "And I want you to know that I'll always be there for you— just like you were there for Grandma Rose."

Jessie said she realized, as she said good-bye to her mother, how fleeting life is, how quickly it passes. Her mother's death made her resolve to appreciate the gift of being alive. That sense of life's brevity and transience is expressed beautifully in the following story, which I found in a wonderful compilation of stories called *Soul Food: Stories to Nourish the Spirit and the Heart:* When a tourist came to visit the famous Polish rabbi Hafez Hayyim, he was astonished to see that the rabbi's house was one small room piled with books. The only furniture was a table and a bench.

"Rabbi, where is your furniture?" asked the tourist.

"Where is yours?" replied Hafez.

"Mine? But I'm only a visitor here."

"So am I," said the rabbi.

Reflections Before Good-bye

I wrote this book to teach other people the valuable lessons of the Four Things, yet in the process my own understanding of them has also deepened. In realizing the remarkable impact that the examples of people working to complete relationships can have on young and old alike, I've come to understand that the Four Things hold essential wisdom for us collectively, across generations.

Perhaps every generation to some extent blames the older generation for making mistakes that affected their lives. As I watch many of my own generation, the baby boomers, dealing with our aging parents, sometimes I hear echoes of adolescent struggles, old frustrations, resentments, and unresolved anger. Boomers' parents have been called the Greatest Generation, and it may be true. They made many sacrifices, endured hardships, and yet worked hard to achieve all they could. But it is also true that none of our parents were perfect.

It turns out, neither are we. Parenting has been (remains) a humbling experience. As my own children enter adulthood, only now do I fully grasp the job description. Fortunately, for us all, being a good parent doesn't require being perfect. This makes practicing forgiveness, appreciation, and love so important. Boomers have the opportunity to reconcile and strengthen our relationship with the Greatest Generation.

Generations communicate largely through the medium of politics. Debates over taxes for things like public schools, health care, housing and retirement, and Social Security tend to dominate intergenerational discussions. By and large, relations between the Greatest Generation and the boomers have been good. We baby boomers grew up in the prosperous post–WWII era, bathed in generosity, showered with advantages by our parents. Things got a little shaky during the Vietnam war, but mostly, both generations have let those bygones be bygones.

Now, of course, boomers are in charge of things in private and public sectors of society, and it's our turn to give back. In fact, how well we care for the most frail and elderly people in our society is the central social and moral test my generation will face. And it's not going to be an easy test to pass. We face unprecedented challenges that our parents could not have foreseen or prepared us to encounter.

A tidal wave of social need related to aging, illness, and caregiving is headed in our direction. Our ankles are already wet. For the first time in human history, in the third

millennium there will be more old people than young people on the planet. In addition to the graying of the popula-
tion, boomers have been far more mobile than our parents
ever were. We often live many miles from our parents and
in-laws. We have smaller families. Many of us work multiple jobs to make ends meet. There are fewer potential caregivers with whom to share the care. The advent of chronic
illness, which is, after all, an invention of the late twentieth
century, adds to the challenge. Throughout the ages people
have died quickly of heart, liver, lung, kidney disease, or
cancer. Now people often live reasonably well with those
illnesses for years, protracting the last phase of life. These
trends are converging to create the perfect storm, a social
tsunami of caregiving need that threatens to overwhelm
our children's generation and us.

We must rise to these challenges. It will take creativity,
collaboration, and an unwavering commitment, but we can
do it. As we care for our parents and as they die, we become
the next generation in line to face the end of life. The models of care we build today will determine the quality of care
we receive tomorrow. It behooves us to nurture forgiveness, gratitude, generosity, and love in ourselves—and
model these qualities for our children.

Personally, in the two years during which *The Four Things
That Matter Most* has gone from an idea to a manuscript
these statements have worked on me in unanticipated, mar-
velous ways. As "Please forgive me," "I forgive you,"
"Thank you," and "I love you" resonated within me, they

gradually became a continuous practice—a meditation. Each statement became a Zen-like tool for being mindful of the qualities of forgiveness, gratitude, and love. In *practicing* the Four Things as an attitude to be cultivated, they have begun to transform my relationship to the world and experience of life.

It's not easy to maintain this attitude for long and I'm still working on it. (They call meditation a practice for a reason.) I'm not "enlightened," but it has been *en-lightening* and enlivening to let go of old baggage, to wipe clean the emotional slate of old debts and grudges.

These generational and personal lessons seem entwined. Mahatma Mohandas Gandhi once advised, "We must become the change we want to see in the world." Perhaps if we were each to expand forgiveness, gratitude, and love in our own lives, the collective influence of our healthy, loving relationships would reverberate across our generations and into the future.

For myself, I've decided that by continuing to practice the Four Things, my relationships will, hopefully, grow stronger and more loving. If I can become the change I wish to see, my friends and family may take notice and respond in kind. And maybe, by earnestly practicing forgiveness, gratitude, and love now, I'll be adept before it's time to say my last good-bye.

Acknowledgments

This book celebrates the people whose stories it tells, as well as the many whose stories would not fit within these covers. I am thankful for the generosity of numerous people who shared their family's story. Each one informed my writing. In every case people I interviewed expressed hope that their experience would be helpful to someone else. I've tried to convey faithfully the essence and lessons of their experiences. In most stories I used pseudonyms and altered details of events to preserve families' privacy.

I am deeply grateful to several people who were instrumental in developing this book from an idea to reality.

Yvonne J. Corbeil contributed to every phase of this project and every aspect of this book. Yvonne's wisdom is woven within these pages. Her penetrating and nuanced understanding of the human experience continues to expand my own. She patiently read draft after draft of sections and chapters, and her instincts, insights, and honesty made each successive draft better.

Gail Ross is my literary agent and good friend who thinks with her head and meets the world with her heart. She immediately grasped the potential in my idea and wouldn't let go. Her excitement and her noodging kept me on track. Jennifer Land's skillful editing helped polish the book proposal.

Kenneth Wapner is a master craftsman of words; a surgeon whose knife leaves no mark. Kenneth's keen appreciation for the rhythm of narrative transformed this manuscript and made it all it could be.

Leslie Meredith, my editor at Free Press, understood that the wisdom of the Four Things was applicable to any time in life and ensured that *The Four Things That Matter Most* remained a book about living.

I am grateful for the personal support I received during the long months of writing from key people in my life.

Carol Parks manages my work schedule and somehow found and protected times for me to write amidst the frenetic swirl of responsibilities and appointments.

My coworkers at the Life's End Institute in Missoula and at the Promoting Excellence in End-of-Life Care office at the University of Montana were generous in their support and flexibility. I especially thank Jeanne Twohig for her patience, encouragement, and enthusiastic support.

I cannot adequately thank my mother, Ruth Byock, and my sister, Molly Byock, for their loving support through thick and thin and for their steadfast excitement for my work.

I appreciate my colleagues Rosemary Gibson and Vicki Weisfeld at the Robert Wood Johnson Foundation who consistently offered their encouragement and support.

I thank my daughters, Lila and Satya Byock, for their love and patience—and for the years of on-the-job training in fatherhood.

Finally, I was blessed with a number of people in my youth who taught me about life and relationships by their words and by the examples they set.

My father, Seymour Byock, was my first instructor in psychology. Dad was as astute an observer of humankind as anyone I have ever known.

Harvey Horne, a gifted psychiatrist, was a mentor to me and a good friend during my formative professional years.

Edith and Norman Glikin, my cousins and auxiliary parents, always epitomized the word *mensch*.

Kay Huntington, Mary Mendel, and Betty Fornataro, the mothers of three close childhood friends, took an interest in me and extended some mothering when I needed it. They helped teach me what matters most in life. I have never forgotten you!

Index

Index

Polansky family, 18–21, 25
Positive legacy, establishment
    of, 56–57
Prayer, 16
Precious Garland (Nagarjuna), 185
Prostate cancer, 70–71

R

Reconnection, unexpected grace
    of, 113–118
Resolution, sense of, 47–48
Responsibility
    creative, 132–133
    principle of shared, 93–94
Rilke, Rainer Maria, 152
Rinpoche, Sogyal, 37

S

SARS, 184
Schumann, Daniel, 176–177
Self-care, 76–77, 133
Self-forgiveness, 48, 78–86
September 11, 2001, 33, 182
Sexual abuse, 40, 69, 72–76
Shared responsibility, principle
    of, 93–94
Sherman, Grace, 114–118
Smoking, 88–89
Social Security, 93
Solitary confinement, 16
*Soul Food: Stories to Nourish the
    Spirit and the Heart*, 212
Stating the obvious, 4–5, 12, 13,
    113

Statler, Alex, 114, 116, 117
Statler, Laurie, 114–118

T

Teresa, Mother, 97
"Thank you." *See* Gratitude
Thoreau, Henry David, 171
Thrombotic thrombocytopenic
    purpura (TTP), 166
*Tibetan Book of Living and Dying,
    The* (Rinpoche), 37
Tillich, Paul Johannes, 35
Trailing adaptation, 81
Transformations, 26–33
Tuesdays with Morrie, 81–82

W

West Nile virus, 184
Whitman, Horace, 148–152
Whitman, Louise, 148–150,
    152
Whitman, Mike, 148–151
Whittier, John Greenleaf, 1
Wiesel, Elie, 118
Williams, Betty, 179–184
Williams, John, 179–184
Williams, Matthew, 179–184
Wills, 195–196
Words, healing power of, 9–17

Y

Year to Live, A (Levine),
    100–101

About the Author

IRA BYOCK, M.D., is a palliative care physician, leading medical authority, and longtime public advocate for improving care through the end of life. He is past president of the Academy of Hospice and Palliative Medicine.

Dr. Byock is cofounder of Life's End Institute: Missoula Demonstration Project, Inc., a community-based research and quality improvement organization focused on end-of-life experience and care. He heads the national Promoting Excellence in End-of-Life Care program for the Robert Wood Johnson Foundation. He is director of palliative medicine at Dartmouth Hitchcock Medical Center and a faculty member of Dartmouth School of Medicine.